Working with Parents of SEN Children After the Code of Practice

Edited by Sheila Wolfendale

David Fulton Publishers
London

David Fulton Publishers Ltd
The Chiswick Centre, 414 Chiswick High Road, London W4 5TF
www.fultonpublishers.co.uk

First published in Great Britain in 1997 by David Fulton Publishers

David Fulton Publishers is a division of Granada Learning Limited, part of Granada plc.

British Library Cataloguing in Publication Data
A catalogue record for this book is available from the British Library.

ISBN 1-85346-429-5

Typeset by Textype Typesetters, Cambridge
Printed and bound in Great Britain

Contents

Home and School – A working Alliance

This Series, edited by *John Bastiani* and *Sheila Wolfendale*, brings together wide-ranging contributions which

- are written from both professional and parental viewpoints
- offer an assessment of what has been achieved
- explore a number of problematic issues and experiences
- illustrate developments that are beginning to take shape

It will appeal to those with a special interest in and commitment to home–school work in all its actual and potential facets

Early titles are:

Working with Parents as Partners in SEN
Eileen Gascoigne
1–85346–375–2

Home–School Work in Britain – review, reflection and development
By members of the National Home–School Development Group, edited by John Bastiani and Sheila Wolfendale
1–85346–395–7

Home–School Work in Multicultural Settings
Edited by John Bastiani
1–85346–428–7

Working with Parents of SEN Children after the Code of Practice
Edited by Sheila Wolfendale
1–85346–429–5

Linking Home and School: Partnership in Practice in Primary Education
Hugh and Jenny Waller
1–85346–482–1

Notes on the contributors

Sally Beveridge is a Lecturer in education at the University of Leeds, where her work includes courses in special educational needs and in home–school partnership for students on initial and post-experience course of teacher training. She has previously taught in both mainstream and special schools and has also worked as a project director of a fully integrated preschool service for children with SEN and their families.

Anna Conrad was a primary school teacher before training as an educational psychologist. Her MSc dissertation focused on the GEST-funded Parent Partnership Schemes. She now works as an educational psychologist in Essex.

Teresa Furze has worked as a teacher in primary, secondary and special schools and as an educational psychologist in Enfield, Barnet and Essex. She is currently seconded as senior project consultant with the Senjit Partnership Consortium of eight LEAs which has also done work for three other LEAs.

Vincent McDonnell has a wide range of experience in working alongside families and pupils with special educational needs. Having taught in residential special schools for pupils with both learning and behavioural difficulties, he first moved into education administration with Sheffield City Council as a Secondary School Officer. He subsequently moved to Staffordshire as Assistant Education Officer for special needs, and is now Principal Officer for all Pupil and Student Services. A member of the Society of Educational Officers National Council, Vincent McDonnell acts as secretary to their Special Needs Committee. On behalf of the SEO he contributed to the implementation of the Code of Practice and Chaired the Steering Committee that had oversight of the Coopers & Lybrand research into the management of budgets for pupils with special educational needs.

Robina Mallett's views on partnership are the result of a mixture of experiences: assisting and advocating for her own children; supporting other parents whose school age children have special educational needs; sharing in the management of a GEST funded parent-led support group – one of whose aims is to 'encourage parents and professionals to work more closely together in the interests of the children'; and, latterly, in a paid capacity (i.e. among professionals) supporting families who have a relative with a learning disability.

Alice Paige-Smith is senior lecturer at the University of Hertfordshire, tutor at the School of Education, the Open University, a council member of the Alliance for Inclusive Education and an adviser for IPSEA. Experience of working in inner-London schools as a support teacher at a primary school, a class teacher at a special school. She has also been an advice worker at the Advisory Centre for Education and an education researcher at the School of Education, the Open University.

Phillippa Russell is director of the Council for Disabled Children, at the National Children's Bureau. She is also seconded on a part-time basis as an associate director of the National Development Team for people with Learning Disabilities. She is a member of many committees and working groups. She was awarded the OBE in 1988 and the Rose Fitzgerald Kennedy International Centenary Award for Women who have made a major contribution to the lives of people with learning disabilities, on the occasion of Rose Fitzgerald Kennedy's hundredth birthday in 1990. She was awarded an honourary doctorate from the University of Southampton (King Alfred's College) in November 1991.

Last and by no means least, Philippa Russell is the parent of a young man with learning disabilities and has been closely associated with a wide range of parent organisations and the voluntary sector over the past years. She is also the author of a wide range of books, articles and chapters on all aspects of disability and special educational needs. *The Wheelchair Child* won the Oddfellow Social Awareness Book of the Year in 1987.

Katy Simmons is the co-ordinator of IPSEA, the Independent Panel for Special Education Advice. Her work includes advice giving to parents of children with special educational needs and representation of parents at the SEN Tribunal. Formerly a lecturer in special education, she has published extensively on special education issues. She writes regularly for professional journals and for the national press and is a regular contributor to conferences, radio programmes, workships and professional meetings.

Sheila Trier has enjoyed considerable experience as a generic educational psychologist in Lancashire and currently with the Devon County Psychological Service. In this role she has been actively involved in developing and maintaining many different training and support programmes for both professionals and parents. Her particular interest in the Early Years has led to promote a model of support for special educational needs which challenges the separation between the worlds of home, school, community and specialist services which can so easily occur. The development of the Parent Partnership scheme in Devon demonstrates the importance of applied psychology as a discipline able to underpin the implementation of practical services which need to acknowledge both the agreements and the conflicts in the perspectives of all participants.

Mollie White is a founder member of the National Portage Association. Her writing and collaborative work with teachers and health professionals has focused on the parents' contribution to the early development of the child. She lecturers in early education at King Alfred's College, Winchester and also works as an independent consultant.

Sheila Wolfendale has been a primary school teacher and remedial reading teacher, an educational psychologist in several LEAs and is currently director of a Doctorate in Educational Psychology training programme at the University of East London. She has authored and edited many books, booklets, chapters, articles and handbooks on aspects of special needs, early years, and parental involvement. She was awarded a Professorship in 1988 and in 1995 gained a PhD by published works.

Note to readers

On November 1st 1996 the 1993 Education Act was repealed. The law on special education will, from that date, be contained in the 1996 Education Act. This is a consolidating act which pulls together the whole of the 1944 Education Act and other subsequent education acts, including the 1993 Education Act.

There have been no changes of substance to the law on special education, although recent amendments to the 1993 Act made by the Disability Discrimination Act 1995 and the Nursery Education and Grant-Maintained Act 1996 have been incorporated.

The 1993 Education Act, Part 3, the law on SEN, becomes Part 4, 1996 Education Act. This book was written before these changes became law, and so readers will find references to the 'old' legislation.

This explanation of the legislative changes was prepared by John Wright from IPSEA (Independent Panel for Special Education Advice, 4, Ancient House Mews, Woodbridge, Suffolk, IP12 1DH) to whom the editor records her grateful thanks.

1 Delivering services for children with special needs: the place of parents

Sheila Wolfendale

The purpose of this introductory chapter is to set the scene, describe the reasons for and rationale of the book, introduce the authors and their chapters and provide commentary on key themes and messages emerging from the book.

Reasons for and rationale of the book

The analogy considered to be most apt is that the book is a barometer, an 'indicator of change' (*Chambers Dictionary*), or to vary the metaphor in the same vein, it is a weathercock, 'showing the way the wind blows' (*Chambers Dictionary*).

The intention is to report upon the early impact of the Code of Practice (1994) within its legislative context, the 1993 Education Act, Part Three, not because such an account can yet be definitive; rather, the authors hope that readers will find it useful to have an *indicative* set of chapters individually and collectively examining the various facets of partnership, as a kind of benchmark.

The book blends a number of ideological perspectives on partnership with descriptions of collaborative ways of working between parents and professionals. It is a celebration of a number of soundly based initiatives that are standing the test of time (e.g. Portage, parents' groups); it affirms the commitment to forging enduring working links between parents of children with special needs and practitioners who work with children or on their behalf (e.g. new and contemporary ventures like the parent partnership schemes); it highlights inherent issues within a legislative framework (e.g. the SEN Tribunal) ; it focuses attention on the main locus where partnership practice should be visible, namely, schools, and it identifies barriers to partnership, while at the same time proposing solutions.

The overall message of the book is a positive and affirming one, namely, that:

- progress towards parent–professional co-operation is evident and increasing;
- commitment to variations on partnership is manifest in a variety of ways.

Yet the authors are nothing if not realistic about the fact that partnership is far from achieved for many parents; too many parents remain unreached and seemingly, unreachable; that the power balance is unevenly weighted towards professionals (teachers, educational psychologists, social workers, health workers, etc.) who too often retreat behind their 'barricades of mystiques' (Midwinter 1977).

The imperative to 'have due regard to' the Code of Practice is not one that can be ignored by schools and LEAs and indeed the recent OFSTED survey (1996) confirmed conscientous and progressive adoption of Code principles and procedures. However, the same survey identified a differential pace in take-up and implementation of these principles and procedures and in respect of parents, the survey noted that many schools had, understandably perhaps, concentrated more in the early days of implementing the Code of Practice, on 'formulating their SEN policies, establishing an SEN register ... having in place improved arrangements for assessing and teaching pupils' (p.25, para.84), than on developing viable home–school links. The survey is a salutary reminder that the principles of partnership with parents are comprehensively articulated in the Code of Practice with practical suggestions offered at each of the Stages to operationalise them.

The authors

Between us, we are parents, education lecturers, educational psychologists, education officers, administrators, voluntary organisation workers – and much else besides, as can be seen from the brief biographical sketches. So we portray an inclusive, multi-faceted approach to the business of 'partnership', optimistic yet realistic, based on collective, profound, first-hand experience and responsibilities.

Organisation of the book

The ordering of the chapters denotes a progression and some continuity between the provisions and statutes of the 1981 Education Act and those of its successor piece of education law in the area of special educational needs, the 1993 Education Act, Part Three (Part Three of this Act is entirely devoted to SEN and constitutes the replacement to the 1981 Education Act). Initiatives described in the first three chapters predate the 1993 Education Act. Mollie White provides a review of Portage which was introduced to the UK in the late 1970s in two areas and which has had subsequent spectacular take-up nationally. Portage had been cited in the Warnock Report of 1978 as an example of good practice, epitomising parent partnership. Robina Mallett gives an account of one post-1981 Education Act initiative in southwest England, contextualised by reference to personal experiences, and Alice Paige-Smith focuses attention on the rise and impact of parents' groups and their lobbying function. Between them, these three authors illustrate graphically the effects and effectiveness of collective groupings of parents. Sally Beveridge's chapter, while concentrating on the relationship between schools and parents post-1993 Education Act, contextualises the notion of partnership by reference back to the Warnock Report. The ingredients for home–school partnership therefore predated the Code of Practice and Sally deals with a number of these main ingredients, refracted largely through the recorded views of parents and teachers.

The ensuing chapters relate specifically to the 1993 Education Act and post-Code of Practice developments. Collectively these four chapters examine early-appearing effects and impact of the new legislation and the Code of Practice. Philippa Russell's chapter is intentionally juxtaposed between the earlier chapters which illustrate continuity and progression in the area of parental participation in SEN procedures and provision and the final three chapters which focus on post-1993 EA initiatives. The chapter by Philippa is pivotal for it picks up on and deals with a number of the key requirements and provisions of the legislation, namely: Named Person, parent partnership schemes, the Individual Education Plan (IEP), the role of the Special Educational Needs Co-ordinator (SENCO), the SEN Tribunal, and school SEN policy.

Teresa Furze and Anna Conrad's chapter provides a wide-ranging descriptive account of the advent and growth of the GEST-funded parent partnership schemes in all their diversity, including discussion of Named Persons and Named Officers, and Sheila Trier tells the story of the setting up, operation and evaluation of one such scheme. The chapter by Katy Simmons reminds us of the legislative context and the double-edged sword that constitutes the SEN Tribunal. The reminder is salutary, for as Katy says (page 125) 'it may be that the existence of the Tribunal is fundamentally at odds with the notion of promoting partnership'. This speculation offered at what is still early days in the Tribunal's existence, brings us back full circle to the checks and balances needed to operate any relationship, and particularly one that is predicated on partnership principles.

The final chapter by Vincent McDonnell initially strikes a cold note of reality when he identifies a number of structural and human barriers to partnership. But he is optimistic enough to think that carers and families should become active partners in determining service delivery, and is of the view that school can play a pivotal role in multi-agency collaborative work.

Themes and messages

A number of themes and messages emerge from these accounts – several of these are now highlighted and discussed.

On partnership

A number of authors have closely examined the notion and feasibility of 'partnership', whether it is or can be *equal*, *reciprocal*, *mutual*, and the nature of differential responsibilities within partnership. Wolfendale posits a number of partnership principles which should explicitly underpin the practice (Wolfendale 1992); Gascoigne (1995) provides a parental perspective and, within a reality-based model denoting constraints upon 'equality', offers options for partnership involving a wide range of education and non-education based professionals. Hornby (1994) conceives of partnership as being a worthy aspiration and cautions 'in order for such partnerships to become more than just lofty ideals, the concept needs to be developed into a formal model for parental involvement designed to guide practice' (p.22); Dale (1996) not only proceeds to analyse and dissect reflectively the concept itself, but also provides a number of highly practice-focused, challenging exercises for professionals to scrutinise honestly the present basis of their work with parents. Not one author, writing on SEN and parents in the last few years, would aver that partnership, as defined, is easy to bring about and, as stated earlier, the chapter authors of this book present the various facets of the relationship.

Would even those academics and practitioners who present a sceptical view of the parent–professional relationship (see below) deny that it is progress indeed when a government publication – the Code of Practice – commits itself to partnership principles? Also, the largest national special educational needs organisation, NASEN (National Association for Special Educational Needs), adopted, during 1995, a policy on partnership with parents and has created a Parents in Partnership Interest Group designed to support the organisation to realise this policy in practice (contact address in references).

Empowerment – equivocal views

There are those advocates of partnership, of whom this author is one, who maintain that a partnership relationship is static and unproductive (particularly for parents) if it does not lead to *empowerment* on the part of parents. That is, unless parents have in reality full and equal rights and opportunities to participation and power-sharing in special needs processes and decision-making, then partnership is not so, and it certainly is not empowerment. An interesting manifestation of empowerment is described by Jordan and Goodey (1996) – they describe the effects of parental pressure upon moves to end segregation of children with special needs/disabilities by making all schools fully inclusive. In describing the evolution, within the London Borough of Newham towards inclusive education over the last decade, they highlight the impact and power of the parental lobby in bringing about such changes.

A number of studies have sought to demonstrate that the powers are stacked on the side of the professionals, that even the dialogue is not open and honest, that the extent to which parents are 'allowed in' is decided by professionals, that arcane bureaucratic procedures persist to the detriment of parents and families at times of stress for them (Galloway *et al.* 1994, Sandow 1994, Armstrong 1995). Sandow, writing later (1995), presages the possible impact of the Code of Practice and hopes that that section which deals with parental involvement gives a positive framework within which relations between home and school can develop' (p.125).

Indeed, as Philippa Russell in her chapter explains, the Department for Education (as it was then), via the GEST scheme (Grants for Education, Support and Training), sought to buttress the Code of Practice rhetoric with the means to foster partnership with parents as a bedrock part of the implementation of the 1993 Education Act, Part Three. Sheila Trier, Teresa Furze and Anna Conrad describe implementation of the parent partnership schemes on the ground.

Objectives for the second year and third (final) year of the scheme (that is, 1995–96 and 1996–97) were couched thus in the relevant GEST circular:

> to encourage partnership between parents, LEAs, schools and voluntary bodies in the work of identifying, assessing and arranging provision for pupils with SEN, particularly but not necessarily all those who are statutorily assessed and have statements of SEN. The development of active partnerhip schemes, including the provision of information and advisory services for parents of SEN children and the identification of 'named persons' is intended to reduce conflict and minimise the number of statutory SEN appeals.

There is no doubt that, at the time of writing (late summer 1996) this scheme which is operating in most LEAs has had significant impact – evidence of this comes informally, even anecdotally at times and from local evaluations of schemes. The key question is whether or not in the longer term, the scheme will have made a difference. That is, will it have brought parents firmly into SEN procedures and decision-making, as equal players; will it lead to empowerment on the part of parents; will it be a catalyst towards the embedding of effective partnership practice on the part of schools? Or will distribution and allocation of finite resources always be a potentially divisive factor, beyond the best intentions of well-meaning administrators and publicly salaried professionals?

A one-year research study (from May 1996 to May 1997) commissioned by the Department for Education and Employment, and under the direction of this author is designed to explore the impact and effectiveness of the parent partnership scheme. The research aims are to:

- identify outcomes and provisions of parent partnership schemes in a range of different circumstances (different LEAs, different types of schemes);
- identify the effects of the schemes upon parents of children with special educational needs as well as upon the LEA, school and other involved personnel;

- identify factors that promote effective partnership practice;
- make recommendations, based on these good practice indicators, as to how parent partnership schemes can be sustained.

(Contact this author at the Psychology Department, University of East London, Stratford Campus, Romford Road, London, E15 4LZ for further details.)

Checks and balances within the system

The education service is coming to terms with legislative imperatives which have increased and safeguarded parents' rights within education and which ensure that schools can no longer exclude parents or ignore the family and community dimension. In the SEN area the Code of Practice is one quasi-legal safeguard. In the broader educational context, OFSTED (1995) sets out the indicators by which schools are and will be judged on the quality and quantity of their home–school links and parental involvement activities. While 'partnership' is not specifically called for in the Inspection Framework, nevertheless the constellation, in sum, of such activities should denote a parent-responsive, parent-sensitive, welcoming approach by schools, on the basic premise that 'by involving the parents, the children may be helped' as the Plowden Report of 1968 put it.

The link between active parental involvement and pupil achievement is the subject of many books and innumerable projects, for example, City Challenge (Wolfendale 1996) and family literacy (Wolfendale and Topping 1996). The presumption that closer home–school ties boost pupil achievement is also a key component in the school effectiveness/school improvement literature – good quality home–school work is on the list of central ingredients (Mortimore *et al.* 1995).

In principle, then, the parents and SEN area should be securely a part of this broader arena and such an inclusive approach to home–school links ought to embrace all parents, including those who are, according to a certain stereotype, marginalised if not alienated from schools for a host of reasons. The challenge for all is to find and apply means of rapprochement to engage and welcome families who could then identify with schools as being relevant to them and their children too.

The needs of parents for support

Another encompassing theme is that of the periodic need of parents and carers for support in the, at times, challenging and stressful job of child rearing. The books mentioned earlier in this chapter (e.g. by Dale, Gascoigne, Hornby) have concentrated upon the needs of parents who have children with special needs. Yet they have, in common with all parents, intermittent if not enduring needs to have access to support for a wide ranging array of parenting tasks and responsibilities and child behaviours (see United Nations 1994, Mittler and Mittler 1994, Beresford 1995 for surveys and discussions on these overarching issues within a context of disabilities and special needs, and the Family Policies Studies Centre 1996 report for the wider context).

The largest survey of parent training and support programmes was carried out by Smith (1996) who looked at over 50 such programmes in the UK. This survey is complementary to the text *Confident Parents, Confident Children* (Pugh *et al.* 1994) which acknowledges these needs on the part of all parents for access to good quality support programmes. Indeed Smith's survey indicated that a number of the programmes take place as part of existing provision offered by statutory services and voluntary organisations and if not exactly yet routine provision, their very existence affirms the need.

It takes a village ... rights and responsibilities

This oft-repeated African proverb 'it takes a village to raise a child' has been used to support the contention that responsibilities for the organisation of children's services is and should be a collective, societal one (Clinton 1996).

Within this equation is the notion that service providers and service recipients are equally *stakeholders* in such community enterprises. Integral to ideas of shared responsibility is mutual accountability, with articulated quality assurance mechanisms, transparent to all and involving all participants. The moves towards such an inclusive approach have been painfully slow, as is evinced by the very need to have a Code of Practice proclaiming the philosophy of partnership, i.e. promoting the inclusive approach. Intrinsic to the notion of partnership in the Code of Practice is close co-operation and co-working between and with other statutory and voluntary services. Exhortations to these services over many years to work more closely together have produced little in the way of reviewing structures, roles, responsibilities, communication networks.

At this present time there is considerable optimism that the Children's Services Plans (CSP) mandatory upon local authority services since 1 April 1996, to co-operate in strategic planning in child-care services, will be a vehicle, its engine rather, to drive co-operative ways of working. The CSPs should be, in future, the core of the local authority's policy on child services. Sutton (1995) provides a review of developments towards CSP and illustrative case studies.

The potential for involving parents and carers in these plans is evinced by a couple of his case studies, and he comments:

> There are special reasons for putting into place comprehensive arrangements for consultative processes with the parents of children with disabilities. Partnership with parents requires clear structures, support for parent and voluntary organisations and an awareness that partnership should be individual and collective in order to feed into the planning process and be part of ongoing evaluation and

> review. Some authorities have already set up parents' and carers' fora to support them in their planning processes.
>
> (Sutton 1995, p.61)

Implicit in these words is the notion of being parent and family-responsive – the United Nations report (1994) referred to earlier stresses the differential needs of families:

> Services need to be planned and delivered in order to respond to these individual needs. Services must not be delivered in inflexible packages or be based on a stereotype of family needs and priorities. These have to be discussed and negotiated.
>
> (UN 1994, p.26).

The Code of Practice, as a blueprint for practice, captures these sentiments. Two years on, can we anticipate steady progression towards visible and enacted partnership practice? The contents of this book aim to describe, convince, inspire, invite others to participate in such challenging processes of service delivery.

The last words in this chapter are taken from a book which initially appears to have little in common with education or special needs matters. In fact, it discusses the philosophy and ideology of a 'welfare state' and, within this conception, certain reciprocal responsibilities and obligations are incumbent upon all of us. These moral imperatives towards one another, and particularly for the sake of our children are what galvanise the moves towards partnership with parents:

> At the heart of the welfare state lies a conception of the just society ... the vitality of the welfare state is a badge of the healthy society. It is a symbol of our capacity to act together morally, to share and to recognise the mutuality of rights and obligations that underpin all human associations. It is an expression of social citizenship.
>
> (Hutton 1996, p.306)

References

Armstrong, D. (1995) *Power and Partnership in Education: parents, children and SEN.* London: Routledge.

Beresford, B. (1995) *Expert Opinions: a national survey of parents caring for a severely disabled child.* Bristol: Policy Press, University of Bristol, Rodney Lodge, Grange Road, Bristol, BS8 4EA.

Clinton, H. (1996) *It takes a Village – and other lessons children teach us.* London: Simon and Schuster.

Dale, N. (1996) *Working with Families of Children with Special Needs.* London: Routledge.

DFEE (1994) *Code of Practice on the Identification and Assessment of Special Educational Needs.* London: HMSO.

Family Policies Studies Centre (1996) *Parenting Problems: a national study of parents and parenting problems.* London: FPSC, 231 Baker Street, London, NW1 6XE.

Galloway, D., Armstrong, D. and Tomlinson, S. (1994) *The Assessment of Special*

Educational Needs, Whose Problem? London: Longman.

Gascoigne, E. (1995) *Working with Parents as Partners in SEN.* London: David Fulton Publishers.

Hornby, G. (1994) *Working with Parents of Children with Special Educational Needs.* London: Cassell.

Hutton, W. (1996) *The State We're In* (2nd edn). London: Vintage.

Jordan, L. and Goodey, C. (1996) *Human Rights and School Change: the Newham story.* Bristol: Centre for Studies on Inclusive Education, 1 Redland Close, Elm Lane, Bristol, BS6 6UE.

Midwinter, E. (1977) The Professional–Lay relationship: a Victorian legacy, *Journal of Child Psychology and Psychiatry,* 18, 2, pp.101–13.

Mittler, P. and Mittler, H. (Eds) (1994) *Innovations in Family Support for People with Learning Disabilities.* Chorley: Lisieux Hall Publications.

Mortimore, P., Hillman, J. and Sammons, P. (1995) *Key Characteristics of Effective Schools: a review of School Effectiveness Research.* London: London Institute of Education, London University (published for OFSTED).

NASEN (National Association for Special Educational Needs) Nasen House, 4/5 Amber Business Village, Amber Close, Amington, Tamworth, B77 4RP.

OFSTED (1995) *Framework for Inspection.* London: HMSO.

OFSTED (1996) *The Implementation of the Code of Practice for Pupils with SEN.* London: HMSO.

Plowden Report (1967) *Children and their Primary Schools.* London: HMSO.

Pugh, G., De'Ath, E. and Smith, C. (1994) *Confident Parents, Confident Children.* London: National Children's Bureau.

Sandow, S. (Ed.) (1994) *Whose Special Need? Some perceptions of SEN.* London: Paul Chapman Ltd.

Sandow, S. (1995) 'Parents and Schools', in Garner, P. and Sandow, S. (Eds) *Advocacy, Self-advocacy and Special Needs.* London: David Fulton Publishers.

Smith, C. (1996) *Developing Parenting Programmes.* London: National Children's Bureau.

Sutton, P. (1995) *Crossing the Boundaries: a discussion of Children's Services Plans.* London: National Children's Bureau, 8 Wakley Street, London, ECIV 7QE.

United Nations (1994) *Families and Disability,* Occasional Papers Series, no. 10, Vienna, United Nations.

Warnock Report (1978) *Special Educational Needs.* London: HMSO.

Wolfendale, S. (1992) *Empowering Parents and Teachers – working for children.* London: Cassell.

Wolfendale, S. (1996) 'The Contribution of Parents to Children's Achievement in School: policy and practice in the London Borough of Newham', in Bastiani, J. and Wolfendale, S. (Eds) *Home–School Work in Britain: review, reflection and development.* London: David Fulton Publishers.

Wolfendale, S. and Topping, K. (Eds) (1996) *Family Involvement in Literacy: effective partnerships in education.* London: Cassell.

2 A review of the influence and effects of Portage

Mollie White

Recognition of the primary role of the parent or carer and the importance of the home environment in the early education of the young child with special educational needs has been one of the most significant achievements of Portage during the last two decades. The Code of Practice (1994) gives explicit recognition to the influence of the home environment on the child's early learning and the rights of parents to a combination of home-based as well as centre-based provision. Portage services are cited for the support they offer to the parent within the home setting and their ability to intervene effectively to meet the needs of children from a very early age.

This chapter explores the background to this change in our perception of the role of parents and the part played by Portage. The material is presented in three parts: firstly, establishing effective parent professional partnerships through the Portage model; secondly, evaluating Portage practice: outcomes for children, parents and Portage services; and thirdly, supporting parent–professional partnerships: implications for future practice.

Establishing effective parent professional partnerships through the Portage model

Why Portage? Background and rationale

Portage was first introduced to this country in the late 1970s into a context where formal education of young children, including children under five with special educational needs had traditionally been concerned with centre-based provision. Increased responsibilities devolving upon families caring for a young child with special needs and the negative outcomes for the family which resulted in themselves triggered early admission to school (Hewett 1970, Carr 1975). The importance of the parental role in the child's development and the need to build on the child's personal environment as the basis for early learning was hardly recognised in the literature devoted to mental handicap. Smith (1986) uses the term 'missing parents' to describe surveys of services provided for mentally handicapped children in the 1960s and 1970s.

Mainstream services provided by professionals such as health visitors without formal training in the field of special needs seemed powerless to support parents when the child presented a recognised handicap. Carr (1975) discussing with families the daily management of their children notes their reports of the sympathy and goodwill extended towards them by professionals visiting them at home but quotes one mother's graphic comment 'they don't know best how to help us'.

Specialist services raised different problems. Warnock (DES 1978) cites the experiences of families caring for young children whose needs required support from a range of clinical professionals. Parents commented first on the number of visits required for consultations on their child and secondly on the sheer quantity of advice they were required to follow.

The Portage model was designed to address the problems faced by such families and the professionals endeavouring to support them.

A model of service delivery

Responding to the gap in home-based provision the Portage model drew on those whose expertise was vital to providing appropriate support (Smith *et al.* 1977). Initially developed in Portage, Wisconsin, the service was conceived as a method through which parents with preschool children with special needs could participate in the educational development of their children (Shearer and Shearer 1972). The model developed in Wessex brought together all those involved with the child's progress: parents, health professionals, education and social services to contribute to a teaching programme tailored to the needs of each individual child and family.

The success of the Portage intervention was measured in terms of developmental gains for the child together with reports from parents on their satisfaction with the service received. Parents participated at every stage of the model which featured the following key elements:

- a regular, usually weekly, visit to the home by a trained home visitor;
- a shared assessment framework which draws on the child's development to establish a profile of strengths and needs;
- shared design, delivery and recording of a programme of teaching activities tailored to the needs of the individual child;
- positive monitoring of the child's progress with regular review;
- a positive management framework which draws on professionals from all relevant disciplines to support the delivery of teaching programmes and to resolve problems raised by families/members of the home-visiting team;
- regular evaluation of service delivery based on changes in the child's developmental profile together with parents' satisfaction with the service received;

- management and advisory support for the service by a team composed of representatives from all the contributing agencies and parents.

The establishment of effective partnerships with parents

The core of this model of service delivery is the close-working partnership that develops between parents and professionals in support of the child. Professional input to the child's assessment is matched by parents' intimate knowledge of their child resulting in an in-depth profile of strengths and needs. Teaching activities building on this profile are designed for the home environment embracing the routines of shared experiences between parent, child, and extended family and friends. Opportunities for naturally occurring practice are thus maximised and the learning achieved is rooted in a meaningful context.

This partnership is further supported through the positive monitoring system which is an integral feature of the Portage model. Ongoing recognition of small-step progress is built into the model and the multidisciplinary forum represented at the staff meeting acts as a resource for the resolution of problems raised by families.

Parents and the Portage teaching technology

The teaching techniques employed by the model are central to the parent-professional partnership. They draw on the sensitive and detailed knowledge of the child both on entry to the project when the initial profile of developmental strengths and needs is established and during the design of teaching activities that build on this profile. At the same time they enable professional expertise and knowledge to be integrated into the long-term teaching plans for each child and the daily teaching activities carried out in the home.

While shared parent–professional assessment and intervention is a feature of good practice in the field of special needs it is not unique to Portage practice. It is the level of parent participation particularly in the negotiation of teaching targets and the design of the individual teaching activity that is unique to Portage.

The Portage activity chart is central to this process. The precision of the directions for writing a Portage teaching activity offers tight control of the teaching process to both parent and professional focused on a shared clearly defined objective for the teaching. At the same time an analysis of the conditions for teaching embodied in the chart offers a set of variables that can be modified to respond to the needs of the individual child and family.

Activities can be tailored to the style of interaction operating between parent and child; the relevance of the family environment; and experiences, materials and stimuli that are motivating for each child and family. They can incorporate desired modifications to the adult–child interaction highlighted by professionals with particular expertise e.g. language or movement.

The chart shown in Figure 2.1 is an example of this process in action.

Portage Activity Chart

NFER-NELSON

Child's name: *Mary*

Home visitor's name: *Jane Roberts*

Week of:

Long-term objective: *Movement 27: Brings both hands to midline*

Week no Chart no. Attained Y/N

Parent activity Y/N Continued Y/N

Teaching objective:
Mary will reach towards mother's face from side-lying position.

Success criterion: 3 out of 5 daily

How often to practise and record: *Whenever you want to play this game. Record first occasion each day.*

Directions: include

	HV	P	P	P	P	P	P	P	HV	P
6		✓	✓							
5		(✓)	✓							
4		(✓)	✓							
3	✓	✓	(✓)							
2	(✓)	(✓)	(✓)							
1										
Days	*Tue**		*Wed*	*Thu*	*Fri*	*Sat*	*Sun*	*Mon*	*Tue*	

* First day of teaching: double column here indicates that both parent and home visitor carry out the activity with the child.

Materials:
Bed/soft blanket on floor

Presentation:
Place Mary on her side on a blanket or in the centre of a large double bed. Lay down beside Mary with your face on a level with hers and close enough for her to reach you. Take hold of Mary's fore-arms and guide her hands to touch your face. Blow on her palms or kiss her hands before releasing them. Wait and watch for Mary's response.

Teaching context:

Success procedure: *If Mary moves her hands towards your face, reward her as above, letting Mary feel your face and lips.*

Teaching procedure: offering help
If Mary ignores you take hold of her fore-arms as above, releasing them as soon as the hands touch your face. Reward as before.

Method of recording:
✓ Mary reaches towards mother's face independently
(✓) Mary needs help to reach out

Acknowledgement: from *The Guide to Early Movement Skills*. © 1994 While, Bungay and Gabriel. Reproduced by permission of the publishers NFER-Nelson.

Figure 2.1 Portage Activity Chart

The important long-term learning objective 'brings both hands to midline' is a priority shared among the occupational therapist, parent and home visitor.

The small step in learning targeted in the chart builds on the therapist's knowledge of the body position *side lying* which will facilitate the desired movement at this stage in the child's development.

The activity chart directions refine the detail of a familiar and pleasurable parent–child interaction to describe precisely how the learning needs of an individual child can be met and a successful outcome ensured:

- holding Mary's fore arms and guiding her hands to touch the parent's face;
- rewarding Mary with a response she enjoys – blowing and kissing her hands;
- setting up an opportunity for Mary to move independently;
- providing support when she needs help;
- identifying a level of response that Mary can achieve independently within a single week.

The concept of positive modelling – *Mary's experience of the activity is always positive* – together with the concept of small-step change – *Mary will increase her independent reaching towards the parent's face as the activity is practised* – provide parents with a simple and powerful teaching tool that can become part of their daily lives. The simplicity of the approach is valued together with the experience of its flexibility to each child and each family.

Within the overall operation of the Portage service the activity chart acts as a record of teaching for all those involved with the child's progress and a source of data for ongoing monitoring and review. Ownership of data concerning the child is thus wholly shared by family, home visitor and Portage team, together with any support professionals working with the child through the Portage service.

Evaluating Portage practice

Outcomes for the child

Successful service delivery was measured both in the United States and the United Kingdom in terms of outcomes for the child. Shearer and Shearer (1972) reported average gains of thirteen months developmentally over an eight-month period for children involved in a study of 75 families receiving Portage.

The Wessex project focused on positive changes in the child's developmental profile as a measure of success. Success in achieving the weekly teaching objectives for activities carried out in the home through the parents provided the supporting data for such change (Smith *et al.* 1977). Teaching objectives covered all areas of the child's development including areas where the child was experiencing the greatest difficulties. Similar results are recorded by Revill and Blunden (1979) who employed a multi-baseline research design to demonstrate an accelerated rate of skill acquisition by children receiving Portage. Figures ranging from 82 per cent to 92 per cent teaching objectives attained were reported.

High levels of successfully attained teaching objectives continue to be reported by Portage services using data from activity charts presented at weekly staff meetings. The importance given to the outcomes of weekly teaching objectives in the monitoring process operating at the staff meeting and the attention given to individual teaching activities affirms the significance of the activity chart design in the teaching and monitoring process.

While the precision of the Portage activity chart supports high success rates it also provides the necessary data for focused discussion of unsuccessful activities at the regular staff meeting drawing on multi-agency staff expertise for suggested action. Cameron (1986) records successful outcomes from such discussion in the majority of cases. Failure to set realistic goals and provide successful experiences for the child can cause stress and tension within the family (Wiehl and Barrow 1987). Clare (1993) draws attention to the need for vigilance in this area noting concerns of families with a profoundly and multiply disabled child. Dessent and Fergusson (1984) suggested a more sensitive profile of development could support parent observation of subtle changes in the behaviour of the multiply disabled child. The focus of the teaching programme then becomes an analysis of the conditions in which the behaviour occurred and the management of these conditions in response to the child's daily experiences.

The home visit

A report from HMI following the establishment of Portage services during the late 1980s supported by Education Support Grant funding gave positive endorsement to the Portage model (HMI 1990). Observations of Portage home visits and an analysis of the features supporting quality teaching and learning were a major focus of the inspection of thirteen newly established projects. The following features were noted by the report as characteristic of good home visits in 62 of the 71 visits observed:

- warm initial greeting between family and home visitor;
- positive references to past and present successes;
- negotiated clearly modelled activities with attention to use of appropriate language;
- involvement of the parent in understanding the progression of learning and the long-term aim of specific small-step activities;
- use of the home environment and materials familiar to the child;
- value placed upon the parents' contribution;
- quality of trust existing between parent and home visitor;
- respect for the parents' culture;

- integration of Portage model into family life;
- contribution of range of professionals to teaching programmes;
- home visitor's knowledge of child development as context for discussion of teaching programmes.

All thirteen projects surveyed were considered effective and some work of very high quality was seen.

Outcomes for parents

Parents' reports on their satisfaction with the service they receive have been a feature of the delivery of Portage services in the UK (Smith *et al.* 1977, Daly 1985). Initially data collected from parents through the use of questionnaires related primarily to the teaching method employed by Portage services e.g. parent involvement in assessment and their participation in decisions concerning the teaching activities.

Later these questions were extended to include service-related issues e.g. the content of the support offered to families outside the design and monitoring of the teaching programmes (Clare 1993, Cappell 1995). Asked to comment on 'things they valued most in a Portage service', parents reported on the diversity of support available from the service through the Portage home visitor (Barker and Keleher 1986). The following items occurred most frequently:

- regular contact with a caring person;
- teaching method approach;
- access to toys and equipment;
- liaison with other services and agencies;
- encouragement and reassurance;
- opportunities to meet with other parents.

Evaluation here highlights the role of the Portage home visitor outside the shared design and delivery of teaching programmes. For some commentators the 'non-Portage' activities are seen as the major source of family support (Dessent 1984).

Daly (1985) addressing this issue cited parents' emphasis and respect for the practical 'getting on with the job' aspects of Portage as an essential context for the relationship that develops between the family and the Portage home visitor. Parents are secure in knowing that they can choose whether to share their feelings and day-to-day problems.

Recognition of these elements of Portage practice is given in the framework adopted at Portage staff meetings where agency and family problems reported by families are addressed. Cameron (1989) comparing the number of problems reported by 100 families receiving Portage services with a parallel group of families caring for a young child with special needs found a lower incidence of reported problems in the Portage group. He suggests that it is likely that the practical help brought to parents through the Portage service pre-empted many problems. At the same time the opportunity to share and report problems as they occurred and to access a network of support through the Portage service resulted in the resolution and alleviation of many such problems and a reduced incidence of the factors associated with family breakdown reported by Hewett (1970).

The powerful coping strategies used by families in responding to their problems noted by Cameron (1989) find echoes in reports from parents on their own experience (Lloyd 1986, Hawkins 1990, Sharratt 1990). Opportunities to share these experiences with other parents both locally and nationally are important to the individual family and to the process of developing support networks (Cameron 1988). Mindell (1988) reported changes in parental attitude following involvement with Portage. Attitudes to their children's potential and to themselves as parents were investigated and compared to those of parallel control groups. Portage parents were considerably more positive in their expectations of their child and of themselves as parents. Clare (1993) comments on parents' reports of greater understanding of their child's difficulties and their ability to help their child.

Outcomes for Portage services

One of the aims of the evaluation of the Wessex project was to provide a clear model of service delivery capable of easy and successful replication elsewhere in the UK (Smith *et al.* 1977). Professionals whose experience included work with families and children within the three major agencies: health, education and social services were seconded to the project to act as home visitors or in the supervisory role as part of their time. The service benefited from the resulting diversity of professional expertise and costs of delivery were shared between the contributing agencies. A management team composed of representatives from all the contributing agencies together with parent representatives was responsible for the service. Training of staff in the use of the Portage teaching model was provided through attendance at a Portage workshop followed by ongoing supervision at the weekly staff meeting.

Figure 2.2 shows how time allocated to each family is the variable influencing the roles of service personnel.

An examination of the dissemination of this model and the development of Portage services over time illustrates both the robust nature of the Portage system of service delivery and the ongoing commitment of Portage services to its long-term maintenance. At the same time it highlights developments in Portage practice arising from changing conditions in the field.

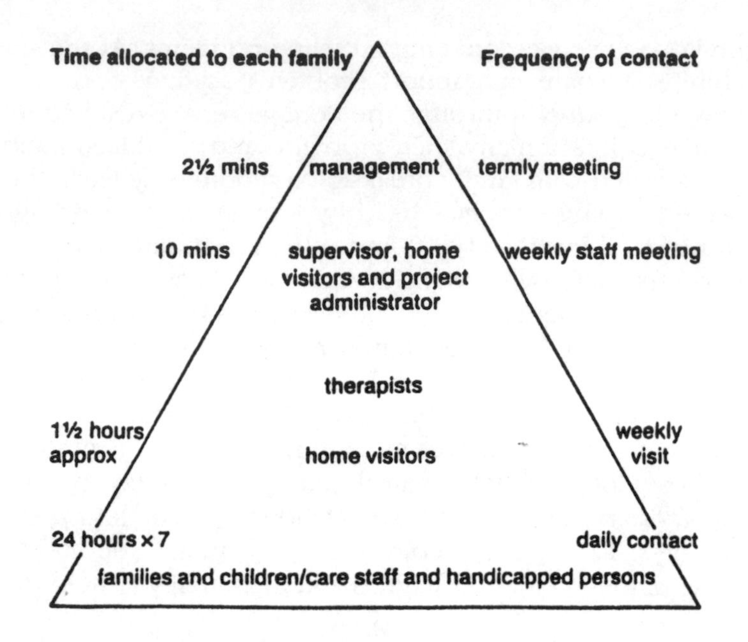

Acknowledgement: from *The Portage Early Education Programme.* © CESA 5, White and Cameron. Reproduced by permission of the publishers NFER-Nelson.

Figure 2.2 The Portage time pyramid

Initial dissemination of the Portage model

Initial dissemination through the literature and the development of training workshops led to the establishment of a substantial number of new projects based on the Wessex model. A follow-up survey of these projects by Bendall, Smith and Kushlick (1984) identified 64 services satisfying key Portage criteria: the use of the Portage teaching methodology in the home setting supported by positive monitoring of multi-professional staff practice through regular team meetings.

Reports of results obtained by these new services (Cameron 1982, Dessent 1984, Daly 1985) stimulated considerable interest in Portage home visiting as a model of support for preschool children with special needs and their families at both local and national levels. Two major initiatives occurred as a result of this interest:

1 the establishment of the National Portage Association (NPA) (Williams 1986);

2 the decision by central government to support the provision by LEAs of 'multi professional "Portage" teams to support parents in the education of children under the age of five years who had special educational needs' (DES Circular 5/85).

The National Portage Association and the dissemination of an agreed model of practice

The development by Portage practitioners through the auspices of the NPA of an agreed Code of Practice and Ethical Guidelines (1986) expressed the concern of the membership to specify and support the maintenance and dissemination of a clear and well-tried model of service delivery. Supported by training workshops delivered by NPA-registered trainers working to an agreed curriculum the Code offers a clear guide to recommended standards of practice. It sets down key elements of practice at all levels of the service: home visit; supervisory and management meetings; and an outline of the role of each participant: parents; home visitors; support professionals; supervisors and management team/advisory group members.

Kiernan's 1992/1993 Survey of Portage Services including those established through Education Support Grant funding reveals that the NPA recommended model of service delivery had been widely adopted and maintained.

Multi-professional involvement with Portage services

The appointment of full-time Portage workers by LEAs funded by Education Support Grants resulted in a significant shift in the composition of Portage teams. Moving from a strong representation of health professionals as Portage home visitors, over 50 per cent in the 1984 Portage Survey (Bendall *et al.* 1994), Kiernan quotes figures of 14 per cent services employing nursing staff, 15 per cent health visitors, 12 per cent therapists as home visitors in his 1992/1993 survey. Despite this shift the involvement of medical therapists continues to be a firmly established element of present practice through shared home visits and participation in Portage staff meetings.

Table 2.1 Involvement of speech, occupational and physiotherapists with Portage teams

	Speech	Occupational	Physiotherapists
Involved with team	142 (99)	125 (87)	140 (97)
Attends staff meetings	85 (60)	74 (6))	88 (63)
Attends home visits	108 (76)	82 (67)	105 (75)
Attends clinic visits	57 (40)	50 (41)	47 (34)

Note: parentheses give percentage of teams where therapists involved attend staff meetings etc.

Source: figures are taken from Survey of Portage Provision 1992/1993, report by Chris Kiernan for the National Portage Association.

Funding of Portage services

One of the outcomes of Education Support Grant funding is the number of services wholly dependent on one source of funding: the LEA. Kiernan (1993) quotes 52 per cent using data returned by 147 services with LEAs acting as joint funders with health authorities and social service departments in a further 35 per cent. Perceived lack of long-term security reported by many Portage services in relation to future funding whatever their source is a continuing concern.

Recognition of Portage home visiting as a desirable component of local preschool services by the Code of Practice associated with Part Three of the 1993 Education Act has improved the long-term prospects for these services but the need for vigilance in regard to funding continues. Current budgetary constraints imposed on LEAs and the unknown impact of funding for preschool services offering support to young children with special needs brought about by the proposed nursery voucher scheme can only add to funding concerns. While the inclusion of Portage services in the initial piloting of the voucher scheme can be seen as a welcome recognition of home-based provision, it raises questions on the relationship of SEN and core funding. Moreover the drive to maintain existing Portage services can mask the shortfall in the availability of home-based provision to children in many areas of the UK reported by Kiernan (1993). For such families Portage services are not an available choice.

Future support for the Portage model of service delivery

The introduction of formal registration of services by the NPA in 1994 is an important mechanism in the long-term maintenance of agreed standards of service delivery. Minimum criteria for registration are:

- families receive regular (at least fortnightly) visits from their Portage home visitor;
- all Portage home visitors have completed a recognised Portage basic workshop;
- checklists are used regularly for initial and ongoing assessment;
- teaching activities are regularly modelled for parents by the Portage home visitor;
- written teaching instructions (activity charts/diaries) are left for parents to encourage recording of daily activities.

At the same time ongoing dissemination of the model is advanced through extensive participation by Portage services in the Association's programme of training opportunities in particular the Training for Trainers' Workshop. Family and professional access to local basic Portage workshops is greatly enhanced as a result of this important initiative.

Parent–professional partnerships and their implications for future practice

Parents' knowledge, views and experience are cited as vital to effective assessment and provision by the Code of Practice in one of five key principles governing the Code. The central contribution of parents to Portage provision over 20 years offers valuable insights into the conditions necessary to maximise this vital role. In this final section I propose to discuss elements in the process supporting the Portage parent–professional partnership and their implications for general provision for under fives with special needs.

Partnership in referral: early identification of need

Despite the attention given to early identification of need in both the 1981 and the 1993 Acts of Education there remain many children whose needs are not recognised prior to school entry. In many cases parents' concerns about their child's development have gone unreported through lack of awareness of available support from a range of preschool services including home-based provision. Collaboration between the various statutory and voluntary agencies following the recommendations of the 1993 Act to produce an overall picture of available services and relevant access points can offer a valuable guide to parents in their search for appropriate support (National Portage Association 1996). Dissemination of these materials to all parent groups in particular non-English speaking families is an urgent future priority for all preschool services.

Partnership in assessment: positive approaches to assessment

Effective assessment is assessment that works for all those involved: child, parent and professional. It will produce a working partnership wherein *reciprocal exchange of information on the basis of equality is integral* (Wolfendale 1995).

The use of assessment to investigate individual developmental progress with the aim of establishing starting points for teaching is the beginning of parents' involvement with Portage services. Participation in this formative process – in Portage terms the identification of acquired and emerging skills and understanding – is for many parents not only their first real opportunity to share their knowledge of their child but also their first positive experience of assessment. One parent put this very succintly '*No one before has ever asked me what Matthew could do – they only seemed interested in his problems.*' The process of sharing in discussion of the conditions in which particular skills are observed gives parents a context for their child's learning and their part in it. Value is placed upon the child's progress and the parents' role from the outset.

In a different context preschool centres and schools who include in their entry procedures an opportunity for parents to participate with their child in producing a record of their child's development and progress through the use of a document such as 'All About Me' report very favourably on the positive outcomes for the relationship between home and school that follow (Wolfendale 1990). Parent involvement in a shared response to any future concerns on their child's progress is greatly facilitated by this approach.

Partnership in assessment and review: sharing the curriculum

Traditional assessment tools used by professionals have limited application to the parent in the home setting. Accessible, sensitive and user friendly materials covering all aspects of early development are a high priority if we are to support a greater number of parents to participate fully in shared assessment. The use of developmental schedules such as the Portage checklist (Bluma *et al.* 1976) is welcomed by parents. Ideally such materials will set up a dialogue between family and professional that supports an understanding of the child's future learning needs.

The Guide to Early Movement Skills (GEMS) (White *et al.* 1994) is an example of Portage-based materials specifically designed for this purpose. Aiming to support parents' opportunities for close observation of the child as the basis for shared assessment and review the sensitivity of the resulting movement schedules to small and subtle changes in the child's movement profile generates realistic and attainable goals for the individual child. At the same time the Guide provides a framework for understanding the place of specific movement skills within the child's overall movement development.

Arguments that parental involvement in assessment and provision is likely to lead to unrealistic expectations for their child in the future are not reported in practice. Portage teaching programmes promote an accelerated rate of progress which parents welcome. At the same time family experience of the process supporting each small step in learning produces a realistic picture of the child's learning needs. Indeed it could be argued that parents who are closely involved in the assessment and review of progress are very realistic about the rate of their child's learning and the conditions needed to achieve results.

While the present population of children served by Portage is a small one these principles apply to the assessment of any child who needs support for learning. Materials designed to support parent involvement in recording observed starting points for literacy development focus on raising parents' awareness of the complexity of the literacy curriculum while highlighting the opportunity to celebrate what has already been achieved as the beginning of ways forward (Rees Shortland-Jones 1994 (*First Steps*), ALBSU 1995, Hannon 1995).

Partnership in teaching: sharing the teaching process

Effective home-based support initiatives are those where time is set aside to share with parents the rationale for recommended practice (Bastiani 1989).

The success of shared reading schemes is a testament to this approach. (Wolfendale and Topping 1996). Portage teaching techniques, such as, the focus on small-step change as part of a longer term sequence; the modelling of desired outcomes; the reinforcement and celebration of each small success, attract positive comment from parents who report their use outside the Portage teaching programme (Boyd 1979, Barker and Keleher 1986). Use of these techniques in the preparation and delivery of Individual Education Plans is well established but their transfer into the home setting once the child enters school is limited owing to severe constraints on staff time. Where local home–school initiatives have provided direct support to the interaction supporting home-based teaching parents report very favourably on their child's progress and their part in it (Copley 1992, Pugh and Poulton 1987, Miller 1994).

Extending the partnership: education for parents

Support for the parenting role as a feature of service provision has been increasingly advocated by policy makers during the last decade (Pugh and Poulton 1987, Pugh *et al.* 1994). While Portage parent–professional partnerships are primarily concerned with the developmental progress of the child, parents report increasing confidence in their parenting role and enhanced parenting skills as a result of their direct involvement in Portage teaching activities. It could be argued that these long-term gains for parents are as important as the child's progress and that the Portage model is an appropriate vehicle of support for a wider range of parents. The following applications of the Portage model respond directly to specific parent needs :

- *The Special Parenting Service* supports the acquisition of parenting skills by parents with learning disabilities. The establishment of personal strengths and needs by parents participating in this service and the negotiation of priorities for their care of their children is a major feature of the successful outcomes reported (McGaw 1993).
- *The Avon Premature Infant Project* used the Portage model as a support system for parents and babies born at less than 33 weeks gestation. First contacts occur before the baby is discharged from the special Care Baby Unit. Ongoing support for the child's progress follows the Portage model and aims to create a positive climate for later development following a pre-term birth (Marlowe 1993, Dolby and Israel in press).
- *Positive Parenting* (Miller 1994) addresses the increasing problems of behaviour management reported by many parents. Aiming first to reinforce parents in their views of themselves as experts on their own children, the course supports experiences which enhance parents' ability to manage behaviour through the use of positive management techniques.

Conclusion

Placing parents first is essential to the future development of services aimed at supporting the young child. The power of parents to participate as equal partners in the cyclical process of assessment, provision and review stems from the relationship they share with their child. It is a relationship at the heart of early development which crosses artificial divides between care and education. Collaboration between the family and a range of outside agencies is supported by ongoing research sponsored by the Van Leer Foundation at the Early Childhood Education Forum into a shared framework for early learning. Aiming to develop a framework which embraces the work of practitioners in a diversity of settings supporting children's growth and development the project begins in the home. It builds on the central principle supporting early learning and development exemplified by families participating in Portage services that:

> care and education are inseparable – quality care is educational and quality education is caring.
>
> (Quality in Diversity Project 1996).

Notes

1. Information on the Quality in Diversity Project can be obtained from Vicky Hurst at Goldsmiths's College, London, SE14 6NW.
2. Information on the NPA can be obtained from Brenda Paul, 127 Monks Dale, Yeovil, Somerset, BA21 3JE.

References

ALBSU (1995) *Read and Write Together: an activity pack for parents and children* London: Adult Literacy and Basic Skills Unit

Barker, A. and Keleher, R. J. (1986) *Parent Evaluation of North Hampshire Portage Service.* Unpublished report available through the National Portage Association.

Bastiani, J. (1989) *Working with Parents: a whole school approach.* Windsor: NFER-Routledge.

Bendall, S. Smith, J. and Kushlick, A. (1984) *National Study of Portage-type Home Teaching Services: a descriptive study of successfully maintained and discontinued Portage type home teaching services.* Southampton: Research Report no 162 Health Care Evaluation Research Team University of Southampton.

Bluma, S., Shearer, M., Frohman, A. and Hilliard, J. (1976) *Portage Guide to Early Education.* Wisconsin: CESA 5.

Boyd, R. D. (1979) 'Systematic Parent Training Trough a Home-based Model', in *Exceptional Children*, 45, pp. 647–8.

Cameron, J. (1988) 'Portage: the parent's voice' in White, M. and Cameron, R.J. (Eds) *Portage: progress, problems and possibilities.* Windsor: NFER-Nelson.

Cameron, R. J. (Ed.) (1982) *Working Together: Portage in the UK.* Windsor: NFER-Nelson.

Cameron, R. J. (1986) *Portage: pre-schoolers, parents and professionals.* Windsor: NFER-Nelson.

Cameron, R. J. (1989) *Parents, Professionals and Pre-school Children with Special Needs: towards a partnership model of problem solving.* Southampton: University of Southampton.

Cappell, A. (1995) *A Survey of Parents' Views.* Ealing: Early Years Support Team for Ealing Portage Service.

Carr, J. (1975) *Young Children with Down's Syndrome: their development, upbringing and effect on their families.* London: Butterworth.

Clare, L. (1993) *Parents' Perceptions of Portage.* London: Huntingdon Portage Service and University College London.

Copley, M. (1992) in Miller, S. and Daly, B. (Eds) *Portage in Groups.* Proceedings of the 1991 Portage Conference, Winchester, Hants. National Portage Association.

Daly, B. (1985) *Portage – the importance of parents.* Windsor: NFER-Nelson.

Department for Education (1994) *Code of Practice on the Identification and Assessment of Special Educational Needs.* London: HMSO.

Department for Education and Science (1978) *Special Educational Needs.* Report of the Committee of Enquiry into the Education of Handicapped Children and Young People (Warnock Report). London: HMSO.

Department for Education and Science (1985) *Education Support Grants.* Circular no. 5/85.

Dessent, S. and Fergusson, A. (1984) 'First Encounters with the Multiply Handicapped' in Dessent, T. (Ed.) *What is Important about Portage?* Windsor: NFER-Nelson.

Dessent, T. (1984) *What is Important About Portage?* Windsor: NFER-Nelson.

Dolby, S. and Israel, C. (in press) *Parent Interaction Programme.* Windsor: NFER-Nelson.

Hannon, P. (1995) *Literacy, HOME and School. Research and practice in teaching literacy with parents.* London: Falmer Press.

Hawkins, W. (1990) *Siblings and Portage – a parents view and experience.* In Proceedings of the 1989 National Portage Association Conference NPA.

Hewett, S. (1970) *The Family and the Handicapped Child.* London: Allen and Unwin.

HMI (1990) *Portage Projects: a survey of 13 projects funded by education support grants.* London: Department of Education and Science.

Kiernan, C. (1993) *Survey of Portage Provision 1992/1993.* National Portage Association.

Lloyd, J. (1986) *Jacob's Ladder: a parent's view of Portage.* Tunbridge Wells: Costello.

Marlowe, N. (1993) *Growing Up After Preterm Birth.* In Proceedings of the 1992 National Portage Association Conference NPA.

Miller, S. (1994) *Positive Parenting.* Newcastle-upon-Tyne: Formword Limited.

Mindell, N. (1988) 'Changes in Parental Attitude Following Involvement in Portage'. in White, M. and Cameron, R. J. (Eds) *Portage: problems, progress and possibilities.* Windsor: NFER-Nelson.

National Portage Association (1986) *Code of Practice and Ethical Guidelines* (a revised version of the Code is in press). NPA.

National Portage Association (1996/in press) Parent Information Pack. NPA.

Pugh, G. and Poulton, L. (1987) *Parenting as a Job for Life.* London: National Children's Bureau.

Pugh, G., De'Ath, E. and Smith, C. (1994) *Confident Parents, Confident Children.* London: National Children's Bureau.

Rees, D. and Shortland-Jones, B. (1994) 'Reading Development Continuum' in Dewsbury, A. *First Steps.* Melbourne: Longman, for the Education Department of Western Australia.

Revill, S. and Blunden, R. (1979) 'A home training scheme for preschool developmentally handicapped children', *Behaviour Research and Therapy,* 17, pp. 207–14.

Sharratt, R. (1990) *The Other Children – what difference does it make?* In Proceedings of the 1989 National Portage Association Conference NPA.

Shearer, M. S. and Shearer, D. E. (1972) 'The Portage Project: a model for early childhood education,' *Exceptional Children,* 36, p.217.

Smith, J. (1986) in Cameron, R. J. (Ed.) *Portage: pre-schoolers, parents and professionals ten years of achievement in the UK.* Windsor: NFER-Nelson.

Smith, J., Kushlick, A. and Glossop, C. (1977) *The Wessex Portage Project: a home teaching service for families with a pre-school mentally handicapped child.* Research Report no. 125, Part I: Report; Part II: Appendices. University of Southampton: Wessex Health Care Evaluation Research Team.

White, M. and Cameron, R.J. (1987) *The Portage Early Education Programme: a practical manual.* Windsor: NFER-Nelson.

White, M., Bungay, C. and Gabriel, H. (1994) *The Guide to Early Movement Skills.* Windsor: NFER-Nelson.

Wiehl, P. and Barrow, P. (1987) 'Portage in Bradford: training volunteers' in Hedderly, R. and Jennings, K. (Eds) *Extending and Developing Portage.* Windsor: NFER-Nelson.

Williams, D. (1986) in Cameron R.J. (Ed.) *Portage: pre-schoolers, parents and professionals. Ten years of achievement in the UK.* Windsor: NFER-Nelson.

Wolfendale, S. (1990) *All About Me.* Nottingham: NES Arnold.

Wolfendale, S. (1995) *Creating and Valuing a Partnership with Parents in Assessment during the Early Years.* Unpublished address to Under Fives Consortium Conference at King Alfred's College, Winchester.

Wolfendale, S. and Topping, K. (Eds) (1996) *Family Involvement in Literacy: effective partnerships in education.* London: Cassell.

3 A parental perspective on partnership

Robina Mallett

In this chapter I look at several types of partnership from a parent's perspective. After considering inherent differences between professionals and parents I refer to factors which affect partnerships between individual parents and the professionals concerned with their child. I do so by describing personal recollections of parent–professional relationships and their impact on me as a potential partner. Next I discuss what can be gained when parents have parent colleagues (and so have partnerships among those who share their role). Finally I outline one model of a parent-led support service which has achieved some broader partnerships between parents and professionals.

I do not discuss here the issue of partnership with the young person whose needs trigger the liaison between parent and professional. This is an immensely significant area. Listening to their experiences (including those of young people who do not use speech), will not only make our adult contributions more effective but will also enable these young people to become the self-advocates they will need to be. Rather I restrict myself to the other main participants: professionals (those who plan and provide services), and parents (who bear and so have a unique, long-term though evolving, sometimes virtually overwhelming love and sense of responsibility for their children).

Foundations for partnership

Current legislation and guidance incite partnerships through encouraging some of the prerequisites. They stipulate how much of the professionals' work should be done with reference to parents. They direct that information should be made available to parents, their views taken account of, their presence at significant meetings valued. Requirements to have a special educational needs (SEN) policy and special educational needs co-ordinator (SENCO) represent great progress in keeping the needs of all children on each school's agenda. Through the promotion of parent partnership schemes (reported elsewhere in this book) there is also awareness that parents may need support to access information and the services provided; the existence of an SEN Tribunal to consider parents' appeals against LEA decisions is an acknowledgement that disputes must be effectively dealt with (see Katy Simmons' chapter).

Despite the criteria governing what should happen, it is apparent that some environments and relationships are supportive and provide what is needed for a sense of partnership to develop, while others engender friction and frustration. The outcomes of these positive and negative experiences are far reaching for all concerned – children, parents/families and professionals. Because of the many costs of bad experiences, to each of these, the parental perspective in any partnership is a subject which deserves honest and thorough consideration by all professionals, who have the main responsibility for setting the style of working relationships.

'Partnership' suggests to me that participants – albeit with different perspectives – are working, with mutual respect, towards a common goal.

While parents approach a situation with their own value system, insight and love for their individual child, professionals operate within a particular context that is influenced by existing theoretical and political beliefs, scale of workload, current budgets and inherited resources, local geographical and cultural factors. Whatever the basis from which stakeholders function, one shared goal is assumed to be that of providing the best possible outcome for the child(ren) under consideration. But of course there may well be differences of opinion about what is achievable, and where and how it should occur.

The most productive, effective conditions for negotiating differences are likely to arise where there is a will to adhere to a shared code of practice, to work at a partner relationship, to listen actively to each other (carefully checking one's accurate understanding of the other's meaning), to present honestly the information which has helped form an opinion, to be flexible, to deal sensitively not judgementally with strong feelings which arise, not to exploit perceived power differentials.

Mutual respect has to be earned, it requires an openness that can be built into systems but also has to be worked on at an individual level.

Endeavouring to build a good relationship with someone who sees things differently to oneself can be extremely uncomfortable; we would prefer to find our views validated by those with whom we work. Some differences in outlook are inevitable given the varying routes by which professional and parents come to their respective roles.

Some differences between parents and professionals

Apart from class and subject teachers in ordinary schools (whose expected involvement in SEN work has recently been expanded) most other educational personnel concerned with individual pupils who have additional support needs have made a conscious decision to take on responsibilities for them. It is different for the parents of such children. Unless adopting a child known to have particular 'extra' needs, this group of parents do not chose the additional aspects of their role. These are unexpected, realised suddenly or gradually, and must be adapted to.

Much had been written about 'chronic sorrow' and the so called 'grieving process' that parents undergo when they discover they have failed to produce 'the perfect child' (e.g. Olshansky 1962). As a consequence many professionals are taught to interpret exhaustion, confusion, frustration, anger or any other 'negativity' from parents, as stages of their coming to terms with a sense of loss associated with their child's 'special needs'. Having observed that adoptive parents who have had advance knowledge of their child's extra needs (so technically cannot have suffered such loss) seem to react in similar ways to being worn out or let down by people and services that they expected to assist their child, I suspect the origins of much parental discomfort have more to do with poor practice than traumatic disappointment in their child! Applying theory rather than exercising empathy may do more to defend a professional than serve a family.

Parents generally want to understand as much as they can about their child's difficulties and the routes through procedures affecting them. They look to professionals for knowledge and advice.

Professionals have read, been taught and guided before and during their passage into their role. Parents have less preparation but learn daily as opportunities arise. Professionals have achieved an assessor's approval, i.e. passed as competent. Parents, even with their multitude of personal qualities, experiences, community contacts and resources are more likely to be wondering 'Why me?'

Both stand to get satisfaction, successes, self-doubts, frustrations, challenges and stress.

The title a professional acquires gives status, recognition of the body of knowledge they have achieved and perhaps reinforces self-confidence. The social standing of a parent of a child with 'special needs' seems to depend, to an extent, on the disability experienced. This can range between 'superhuman' to 'ineffectual parent'. Wherever the judgement rests we may be perceived uncomfortably – other parents feeling sorry for us or suspecting we resent their 'better fortunes'. We are (accidentally one hopes) frequently called 'special needs parents'!

Professionals gain income; parents extra expenditure due to the phone calls, transport requirements, special clothing, equipment, diet etc. related to meeting their child's needs. Through their work professionals could expect a structure to their careers. Parents are more likely to face lost or restricted career prospects due to interruptions caused by appointments, holiday care responsibilities, stress.

Professionals gain colleagues. Certain experiences tend to separate parents of children with extra needs from most other parents. Relations who are also new to disability issues may react negatively, disappoint with the support they offer or the terms they use, thus contributing to the feelings of isolation that families can experience.

Professionals operate on accepted terms and conditions which cover breaks, health and safety, line management, grievance procedures and so on. A parent's relationship with a child with any disability carries societal and familial expectations; generally these are all encompassing and no let up from responsibilities is guaranteed!

In most cases professionals know that others can and will fulfil their role if they do not. Each parent's emotional concern for their child and his/her future is unique. Professionals' engagement ceases by choice or compulsion; parents' engagement changes but does not stop except on death!

All this accounts for a difference in the emotional, social, financial, theoretical and physical bases for supporting children. In turn these affect the perceived and actual power parents and professionals have. Parents are repeatedly reliant on professionals, who can more easily ignore their dependence on parents' co-operation.

It is not intended to imply an inevitable chasm between the two types of involvement. Being influenced by different motivation, knowledge and pressures, both will have their own strengths to offer. Neither are the two groups of people mutually exclusive – some 'parents' are professionals in the educational or human services fields; and since many of the 'professionals' concerned are themselves parents they may be parents of children with special needs, or yet become this through their child's illness, accident, development or life changes.

Very often, when your child has 'special' needs (i.e. additional to those generally expected) you have contact with a great number of professionals. It is every parent's experience that some are enabling and empowering, empathetic and supportive, while others are not. In practice what counts is attitude and the style of working which this leads to.

Attitudes and working styles: a parental perspective

In many ways attitudes and working styles echo the stages in the historical development of the concept of 'parents as partners in education'. Over time there has been a progression from seeing parents as a potential hindrance to professionals (specialists, who alone knew what was best for the child), through considering them as a possible source of assistance to these 'experts', to realising they are central figures of responsibility in a child's life and therefore protagonists in the task of meeting their needs.

While we can fulfil each of these expectations of us, only the last will enable us to operate as partners in the sense that the term partnership suggests to me!

I would like to illustrate the effect of different attitudes and styles from personal experience. I have taken my examples from a health setting for several reasons. One is to give a little distance from the educational contexts in which readers probably work; by doing this I hope you will find it easier to empathise with the parental perspective. Another is that discussion with other parents has confirmed that my experience has elements which are not uncommon; many of us therefore arrive at educational institutions carrying the effect of such incidents with us and you may 'reap the consequences'. As you read perhaps you will recognise similarities with events in your own working environment and link them to the ways you put the Code of Practice into practice.

When she was seven months old we had agreed with our GP's recommendation that our second daughter be referred to paediatric services. She had had several febrile convulsions, was developmentally delayed, had a marked tremor and poor muscle tone.

O was eleven months old when our appointment arrived – almost half her age again since the GP's referral letter. Access to 'treatment' was via an interview with a consultant paediatrician. M, my partner, in the early stages of self-employment, earning very little and feeling under pressure, came with me to the clinic but left after waiting 45 minutes beyond the appointment time.

When O and I did go in to see the doctor he spoke as much to his entourage of students as to me and reached inaccurate conclusions about milestones that O had achieved because he did not verify his impressions with me. After all the waiting the consultation was over in a flash; I went home and tried to explain to M what had happened.

I was invited to bring O to a weekly play session and a few weeks later the occupational therapist asked me how I had got on at the initial appointment. She indicated that I was not alone in feeling as I had afterwards and asked me to accept the next appointment with the paediatrician and use it to explain the effect of his manner. She felt I might manage this when some other parents would find it impossible. Clearly his approach was affecting the relationships that she was trying to offer parents who were at an early stage in their careers as parents of children with substantial additional needs.

So dawned an awareness that parents of children with 'special needs' are frequently on duty as diplomats on behalf of others who follow and must learn to be assertive. We both went to speak to the paediatrician, who was dismissive of what M had to say.

On top of our individual responses to having a child who was clearly making a different sort of progress to our first, our varying reactions to the way we were rudely treated led to friction between us. I resented this, it seemed avoidable at a time when we were already tired, stressed and confused.

The paediatrician wrote to our GP, explaining that he suspected we would not choose to see him again; years later he even had the sign on O's hospital bed altered so that we would not suspect he was the neurologist who would be interpreting her brain scan.

This man's 'them and us' attitude pervaded the working practices of most of the staff at the centre, with consequent repercussions for parents and children.

All other parents succumbed to pressure to leave their children with the qualified staff while I chose to play with and mediate for O, who did not seem to be consistently in touch with what was happening to her, was often frightened and withdrawn (five years later continuous epileptic absences were confirmed). I believed I was seen as insecure and overprotective.

O was taken away to separate physio and speech therapy as if these were treatments I should not witness. I thought I was judged to be suspicious and demanding because I asked what happened in the therapy sessions.

We all felt on edge, I could not trust the staff's opinions, it seemed they felt challenged by me and as a result O was not getting good attention. I went back home to O's older sister worn out and less patient than I wanted to be.

Dissatisfaction with the attitudes and assumptions operating at the child development centre meant that when A, our third daughter, was born showing similar symptoms of some neurological condition, I could not bring myself to take another dose of the same regime and told our GP. He accepted my view of the experience I had had and told me he was sure I had learnt what would be helpful to A through caring for her older sisters.

In time we were offered assistance for A at another child development centre. Here the staff's qualifications and the salary bill must have been similar to those at the first centre but the attitudes and practice were totally different.

The second centre understood a newcomer's need for clarity and information. At the outset all personnel were introduced and the assessment process described; throughout parents were welcomed as a valuable source of information and an essential resource for their children. The whole family was considered and encouraged to contribute to the early appointments.

Partnership and sharing were an integral part of the way all staff worked. After initial individual assessments everyone participated in a discussion. Parents shared their children's play sessions and so were exposed to opportunities for mutual support to occur. We were joined by a dietitian or benefits expert when the need arose. When A had physiotherapy, the speech and language therapist or a music therapist worked with her and I was shown what I could do at home.

Emotions were sensitively considered. I was able to accept praise for A's progress and allowed to weep with the exhaustion and the weight of responsibility that I felt when I thought of my need to do my best for these two girls and their older sister.

This was a different experience, of co-operatively working. One which made me feel supported, and set me up as a positively disposed, potential partner for future relationships with professionals.

Reflections from these experiences

I have thought about these events and realise that elements occur in other settings with similar consequences.

Delays in getting to specialist services heighten concerns; not only do you feel your child is going without something they probably need now but also that there must be great pressure on services, probably due to insufficient resources and so the fear of rationing creeps in with the question 'will we qualify for help?'. Assessments and those who undertake them take on further significance.

Being kept waiting beyond appointment times somehow depersonalises you; not only may you lose your supporter, you somehow become less of yourself in a waiting room! Your child is no longer 'at their best'. You worry about the arrangements you have made in order to get there, (for other children, transport etc.), will these need modifying and if so, how?

Gate-keepers to any service your child may need are inherently powerful. If they demonstrate their attention is split by exposing other agendas it offends you. If they reach conclusions which you know to be wrong, do not take advantage of your presence to check on them or pay attention to all presented evidence, you lose trust in their opinions, feel them to be arrogant and worry about the implications of their inaccuracies. This is extremely uncomfortable; emotional overload leads to anger, a need to tell someone, panic that you have not managed something important well enough and a dread – is it always going to be like this?

The occupational therapist's perceptiveness was welcome; she listened and suggested practical action. However, it was concerning to realise there was a pattern of destructive meetings followed by attempted rescues – how could the staff work effectively amidst this?

Our meetings with the paediatrician were uncomfortable for him too. We were not alone in needing to tell other people about what had happened. Such is the seedbed of rumour and reputations, others get drawn in and prejudices get fed.

When I was excluded from O's therapy sessions I wondered what they were 'doing to' her, asked myself why I was kept out when I was her primary carer and decided they must see me as a nuisance. Aware of the mismatch between our views of the part I could play, I noticed evidence to support my own and concluded the staff were cool with the children. Among all of this I wanted the children's needs to be the priority; I also wished to be liked, sensed the reverse and felt acutely aware of my own discomfort.

The mix of emotions described above may be completely exclusive to me, but when I occasionally hear professionals complain about parents who do not come to appointments I wonder what their stories are. Apparently sometimes the costs of meetings outweigh the benefits.

Good parent–professional relationships are significant and memorable. It was a turning point for me when our GP showed confidence in my ability to do the right things with our third daughter. I felt relief, pleased to sense some approval.

Was it only that I had found and chosen the second development centre that I felt so much more positive about it? I think not.

I really appreciated the thoroughness and thought that had gone into setting up and explaining the structured assessment process. That we were seen as an essential, knowledgeable resource for A meant we felt heard and respected. In turn we could hear and respect the staff. Co-operation between personnel was obvious, we sensed respect and witnessed good communications among the team. Here a child's wellbeing was a priority – we knew our own was safe and would be helped.

It was usual for parents to stay in group play or individual therapy sessions. The staff knew the former could nurture a self-help atmosphere and facilitated this, encouraging us to acknowledge and share what we had already gained from our experiences. These professionals were not threatened by our needs – if they could not help us themselves they brought in others who would. Co-ordinated therapy sessions were fun, made economical use of our time and supplied us with techniques which became an integral part of our day's activities.

Because our emotions were sensitively dealt with it felt safe. We could show, discuss and honestly face our feelings. The whole family context had been acknowledged from the start, it was a tough and complicated aspect of our situation. While good relationships developed so did much else – a sense of being able to manage what was required, trust in the skills of the staff, belief that our children were getting what they needed and that things would be OK.

In these ways our parental perspective is significantly informed by early experiences of dealing with professionals. Each later relationship with them also impacts on us and influences our further expectations and potential participation. Bad practice is remembered.

A full appreciation of what partnership takes, however, means thinking beyond personal contact; though good individual relationships help, they are only one aspect of partnership. For, even though our experiences at the second family centre were effective for A and empowering for us, we were not really equipped for anything beyond the stage we were at. If all we have to go by is our first-hand experience as users of services, most of us will gather little about our rights under the law, guidance and statutory authorities' obligations. This means we will act only as receivers, rather than fully participatory partners, able to influence the services offered.

Like anyone trying to understand and play a responsible part in anything, parents of youngsters with SEN need to have information about the structure of the systems they are dealing with – the personnel and procedures; their rights and entitlements – what they can expect, what it is possible to challenge; plus emotional and practical support to access and use services. They also need effective mechanisms to offer feedback which do not penalise them or their children. Even if aware and willing, professionals can only provide part of all that is needed and the best providers of the rest are probably parent colleagues and voluntary groups.

Parents supporting parents

Warnock (DES 1978) was aware of the part informal support could play. Given the complexities entailed in currently providing sufficient adequately skilled and supported 'Named Persons', in keeping with the Code, it is perhaps understandable that the role was not developed and offered as intended at the time of the 1981 Education Act. It seems more surprising that Warnock's recommendation that professionals should offer parents opportunities to achieve informal, independent support via relevant voluntary groups was rarely acted upon. When self-help, self-advocacy and the view of the client-as-consumer were strong, why did so few professionals find out about and offer information on voluntary support groups?

Many professionals seem wary of what might happen when parents get together. As 'keyworker' to their children, parents have opinions on a range of services and professionals. Perhaps professionals are fearful that parents' views may be critical and become compounded by consensus, in turn damaging professionals or as yet 'naive' parents. Even if such anticipated dangers were to become realised I believe the benefits of having parent-colleagues can outweigh any real or perceived risks.

Having found ourselves in circumstances which, in significant ways, separate us from the majority of parents we can experience an isolation that renders us so anxious and disempowered that we either become the aggressive warrior (fighting all the way) or passive and defenceless against any bad practice.

For those who have access to and choose to use peer support, the benefits are numerous.

With parent-colleagues we can share the time it takes to deal with concerns, time professionals can rarely give. Through sharing our experiences we can give and gain empathy, which provides us with emotional support. (We are more likely to be offered sympathy from parents whose children are developing along more familiar routes.) Conversations can range over numerous topics, helping to put thoughts into perspective and often providing information we needed but did not even know we lacked. Naturally parent-colleagues have much first-hand knowledge about local procedures, facilities and resources, some of which is not known by professionals we meet.

We exchange anecdotes which reflect received practice rather than stated theory and policy. There may be dangers in this, sometimes reports will be misleading, being based on partial knowledge or having become inaccurate in the retelling. As uninformed parents we are as susceptible to such errors as anyone else with insufficient knowledge. Furthermore through listening to others we develop a sense of our own identity within our role: we do not accept unconditionally what any other parent tells us, we discern who we feel inclined to trust. The more parents have accurate information, the more this will be disseminated.

As our children move through each stage of their lives, ongoing access to others with similar responsibilities gives us examples to follow and continuity of support – extremely valuable when services are distinctly age based.

When we speak to other parents we often 'hear' for the first time something a professional has explained before. Whether through increased receptivity to a peer because they are not so likely to have vested interests, a sense of it being safe to ask again or just plain repetition, we can learn what we needed to understand. (Helping unpick each other's fears, for example about funding, a child's loneliness or the extent of someone's authority, can clarify a way forward, indicate what information is needed and where it might be accessed.)

If the same complaints do get amplified through sharing our experiences, surely good practitioners should have nothing to fear? Any criticism inherently implies what would seem better, and for effective services the best methods of delivery must be sought. The vast majority of parents have no ambition to control systems but many could suggest significant, non-costly, improvements.

Professionals may worry about the power of networked parents. Successful lobbying by groups can bring pressure to bear on the resourcing of services. Interest in one group of pupils could lead parents (individually or linked) to make demands on services which were considered unreasonable by those with an awareness of the whole spectrum of needs to be met.

Such destructive competition for attention and resources is less likely to occur where all voluntary groups associated with SEN are encouraged, not only to present their particular view of services to an LEA, SSD (Social Services Department) or Health Authority, but also to share their experiences with other groups. Through forum meetings common complaints, information needs and examples of good practice can be shared and action requested in a collective way.

Supportive Parents for Special Children[1]

Since 1988 Supportive Parents for Special Children (SPSC) has developed a partnership scheme that provides support to individual parents, links different parent groups and has established working relationships with service planners and providers at many levels throughout what was formerly the area administered by Avon LEA.

From the start SPSC has been a joint initiative by parents and professionals, though it has always been parent-led. Having recognised the inadequacy of peer support among parents, professionals who were investigating the training needs associated with the 1981 Education Act, enabled a group to form. Initially they provided a school hall and mailing facilities so that parents could meet. Later they responded to requests for help with training, approaching the education committee and publicising SPSC's existence to all parents whose children were undergoing multiprofessional assessments or experiencing difficulties we may be able to help with. (For a full account of SPSC's origins, by founder members, see Broomhead and Darley 1992.)

Before they formally constituted SPSC, the parents who were brought together were immediately struck by the fact that they had far more in common as a result of their experiences than the range of our children's disabilities might suggest. Some of us had been members of disability specific support groups, but could see extra value in also having an umbrella organisation. This could be valuable to parents who did not identify with existing self-help groups and would combine knowledge and energy. Through discussions with each other we realised how much we had learnt so far, began to see how much we still wanted to find out and felt stronger for sharing our insights. We wanted to help other parents avoid some of the isolation, powerlessness, information seeking and misunderstandings we each seemed to have suffered.

Our daily experiences demonstrated what worked and what seemed unhelpful. Talking together gave us numerous ideas for making improvements to the systems we were involved with.

So, as well as giving help on an individual basis (rather as the Named Person seems to have been visualised), the group was keen to provide feedback to professionals because we aimed to improve things on more than a personal level.

In clarifying things for us, professional members indicated how they had a remit to set up, run, review and develop services to meet statutory obligations. As service planners and providers they needed to communicate their procedures both to users and other operators of these systems. As receivers (directly ourselves and indirectly via our children) we had suggestions to offer about making these activities as effective as possible. For example, in order to assist other parents track and understand any formal stages their children's assessments had reached, we decided it was essential to have copies of all the standard letters that the LEA used. When we read them we could spot which parts caused confusion to the 'lay' readers for whom they were intended; our suggestions for improvements were passed on by our professional colleagues. Parents were soon being invited to review new letters and on to working parties to help write fresh documents.

Following the example of SNAP (Special Needs Advisory Project) in South Wales, we decided to train parents whose children had special educational needs to support other such parents. A two-part training totalling 30 hours was devised and led by two educational psychologists and a social services trainer. This was intended to enable people to come to terms with their own situation and so lessen the likelihood their own experiences would cloud their ability to understand how it feels to be another parent with a different perception of their predicament; to give a basic knowledge of the relevant legislation, local policies and resources, as well as where to turn for more information; and to equip them with listening skills so they can look for the 'theme behind the words' as they talk to other parents. (Dealing with strong feelings, personal safety and potentially daunting situations such as child abuse were also included.) Over the years the training has been amended where necessary and is now published in a manual for others.

Trained volunteers sign a written agreement stressing the confidentiality of the work, specifying SPSC's responsibilities to them and theirs to the parents they support, as well as the organisation. They receive ongoing training, support and expenses.

A great deal of individual help is given to parents via a telephone helpline staffed by a team of trained parents (who receive a sessional fee). All calls are monitored so that the type, frequency and location of difficulties and enquiries can be fed back to LEAs without identifying individuals. (We use a computerised Enquiry Monitoring System, devised by a committee member.) Enquiries are dealt with immediately or referred on to other trained parents for more in depth support if this is preferred.

SPSC facilitates feedback about how LEA (and other providers') services are received in a number of other different ways.

Each term parents' groups concerned with children who have particular disabilities are invited to send a representative to a forum meeting, so any difficulties and successes their members are experiencing can be shared. Key questions are formulated and sent to LEA officers as agenda items for subsequent discussions with a smaller group of these voluntary group representatives. Parents chair and take minutes at these meetings; while some items recur over the years, others do get resolved. These regular consultations provide opportunities for LEA personnel not only to answer particular questions, but also to discuss and disseminate policy to individuals who will share them with other parents.

Termly open meetings are advertised to every school and unit in the area. These address issues concerning parents, but are also well attended by professionals. Generally professionals or councillors are invited to make a presentation and answer questions from the floor, thus encouraging dialogue which could not otherwise occur easily.

Members receive newsletters about meetings, and local and national developments which may affect them. Links with ACE (Advisory Centre for Education), Network '81, Contact a Family, the National Parent Partnership Network and various other parent partnership alliances strengthen SPSC's information base. Membership of FIAC (Federation of Independent Advice Centres) provides indemnity insurance cover.

To celebrate good practice and share the expertise of those who work with them, we also hold 'Differentiation workshops', where parents, governors, teachers and general assistants learn about and try out some of the techniques used to help our children. These are a popular and enjoyable method of spreading useful ideas while modelling partnership.

SPSC promotes the contributions and insights parents can offer.

At gatherings of parents SPSC personnel have elicited and noted what they felt helped and hindered meetings within school, subsequently using the list elsewhere as a prompt for other parents and professionals to review practices.

Whenever possible the group arranges parent representation on working parties undertaking particular SEN-related tasks and advisory bodies overseeing elements of the LEA's work.

SPSC's governor training programmes, on responsibilities associated with the Code of Practice and working with parents, utilise parents as presenters and groupwork leaders. Their content and parental input have been positively evaluated.

A training video has been produced as a result of filming a course of facilitated discussions between parents and professionals who came together to share their experiences of partnership. The costs, benefits, barriers and enablers of partnership are spoken about frankly; we hope the video and training notes will be a valuable tool for stimulating discussion among professionals, parents and mixed groups.

Between 1994 and 1997 GEST funding under the Parent Partnership Scheme has largely covered the costs of SPSC's activities. Before this the organisation was dependent on small grants from trusts and a huge amount of voluntary effort which could not have been sustained. People outside SPSC expressed concern that accepting GEST funding would compromise our independence. However, our negotiated performance criteria stipulate that we are to 'deliver independent advice and guidance services' and we have continued to challenge through our strengthened existence.

Local government reorganisation has brought fresh challenges and possibilities. Like the parents and professionals we have worked with in Avon, SPSC is adjusting to four new unitary authorities. We hope our support groups from each area of the old authority will form a good basis for strong new alliances, that our 'link' workers attached to each new LEA will keep our helpline staff informed of new personnel, structures and procedures so we can continue to give accurate information to parents at a time of increased stress.

Whatever funding is available in future we will encourage local parents to expect to carry on receiving support in building partnerships with those who work to meet their children's needs. For, though each of us knows every day may still bring anxieties and disappointments about the experiences our children meet at school, better partnerships will help reduce the all too frequent wish to ask that fundamental question: 'Would this be good enough for you if it were your child?'

Note

1. While the services offered remain valuable, given the benefits of hindsight and an increased understanding of disability equality, today the same people may well have chosen a different name for the organisation.

References

Broomhead, R. and Darley, P. (1992) 'Supportive Parents for Special Children: working towards partnership in Avon', in Booth, T., Swann, W., Masterton, M. and Potts, P. (Eds) *Policies for Diversity in Education*. London: Routledge in association with the Open University.

Olshansky, S. (1962) 'Chronic Sorrow – a response to having a mentally defective child', *Social Casework*, 7, pp.190–3.

Department of Education and Science (1978) *Special Educational Needs* (The Warnock Report). London: HMSO.

4 The rise and impact of the parental lobby: including voluntary groups and the education of children with learning difficulties or disabilities

Alice Paige-Smith

Introduction

This chapter will explore the notable developments of parent groups and voluntary groups around the country. Examples of parent and voluntary groups will be provided in order to illustrate how these groups operate. The education policy and practice they are responding to, and attempting to change and influence, will be examined.

I see, firstly, the difficulties surrounding the development of the concept of partnership between parents and professionals as inevitably stemming from the unequal power relationships between these two groups, with education policy and practice restricting the rights of parents to participate in decision-making surrounding special education provision. Secondly, I go on to describe the attempt by parents to understand and manage the procedures which have led to the formation of groups which support and inform parents. This will be explored through the perspectives of parents involved in four voluntary groups. These parents set up these groups in order to counteract their isolation, to express a 'collective voice' and to secure resources for their children for either integration or special school.

Finally, I shall consider how these groups are a part of a collection of voluntary organisations and parent groups which support parents of children who experience difficulties in learning or have disabilities.

A brief history of a concept: parental partnership

The 1981 Education Act was based on the recommendations of the Warnock Report in 1978. This report encapsulated the views of the committee members and those who contributed evidence towards the review of education provision for young people who were considered to need 'a more positive approach' to be bought about by the adoption of the concept of 'special educational need' (DES 1978, para 3.6). Nicki Cornwell (1987) recognises that 'there was a small but vocal lobby for parental rights', at least 26 parents of young people with disabilities or learning difficulties were acknowledged as contributors to the report (DES 1978).

The Warnock Report (DES 1978) produced a chapter on 'Parents as Partners' which developed the notion of 'partnership'. This chapter could be considered to have a prescriptive attitude towards parents of children who experience difficulties in learning or have disabilities. Advice and practical help were recommended to come from a professional who should, 'exercise his [sic] skills in alliance with the parents and shape his contribution around the parents' own understanding of what is required' (DES 1978, 9.13).

The report acknowledges a shift towards parental involvement in the multidisciplinary assessment of children and young people categorised as having special educational needs and requiring a statement of their needs and provision. The report recommended that LEAs should provide a Named Person to assist parents and provide support during the assessment process. However, very few Named Persons actually emanated from the 1981 Education Act (ACE 1991).

Shifting forward a few years to the Department for Education's publication in 1994: The Code of Practice on the Identification and Assessment of Special Educational Needs, the notion of the Named Person re-appears in sections 4:70 to 4:73. This time the emphasis is on how the Named Person should be independent from the LEA:

> It is the LEA's responsibility to identify the Named Person when a statement is made. They should always seek to do so in cooperation with the parents. The Named Person should be someone whom the parents can trust.
>
> (DfE 1994, 4.72)

While the concept of support for parents remains, there is the proposition that parents require someone they *trust*. What has happened during the gap in time between the 1978 Warnock Report and the 1994 Code of Practice that requires a Department for Education publication to acknowledge that parents need someone beside them who they can 'trust'? Does this indicate a breakdown in the notion of partnership between professionals who represent the LEA and parents? Perhaps this emphasis on the need for parents to have support and 'trust' is further recognition of the tensions between the views of parents and professionals? The Warnock Report stressed that while independent advice is important for parents they should not be 'presented unnecessarily with conflicting advice' (DES 1978, 17.26).

Parents' rights

From 1978 the term 'special educational needs' was understood to include those children who experience difficulties at some time during their school career – identified to be one in five children. For the approximately 2 per cent of children who require a statement to secure their provision, their education in ordinary school depends upon the 'escape clauses' of the 1981

Act (replaced by the 1993 Education Act); that children's special needs are met, that there is the efficient use of resources and provision of efficient education for the rest of the class (1981 Education Act, 2.3, 1993 Education Act, 160).

However, parents were not given any 'rights' to challenge the decisions made by LEAs in the 1981 Education Act. Instead the power of the LEA to decide on the needs of the child and the subsequent provision was maintained through the multidisciplinary assessment led by professionals. Parents can make a contribution of written evidence of their views on the draft statement under the 1981 Education Act. Under the 1993 Education Act (section 167) parents were given the right to state their preference for the school of their choice in their contribution towards the final statement. As Phillipa Russell (1994) notes, the Code of Practice (1994) was an attempt to introduce a national policy to 'achieve greater clarity and consistency' between LEAs. The Code of Practice does specify arrangements whereby parents and professionals can annually review a child's progress and provision and amend the statement. The introduction of the Special Educational Needs Tribunal in the 1993 Education Act may encourage LEAs to be accountable to the code – only when parents decide to challenge the practice of the LEA which affects their own child. The lengthy waiting list of families challenging LEA decisions at the Special Educational Needs Tribunal indicates the breakdown of partnership between parents and professionals. One parent with Dyslexia considered the tribunal to be an intimidating procedure:

> I could not afford a solicitor and had to represent my own case. This I found extremely difficult as I left school at age 15. Apart from my own academic difficulties in presenting a written case I was so emotionally involved that I made important mistakes. In the booklet it says the tribunal is informal and you do not need legal representation. This is untrue and if I had had a solicitor I feel the outcome for my son would have been very different.
>
> (House of Commons Education Committee 1996, p.32)

The DfEE has acknowledged the lack of partnership between parents and professionals and that LEAs place young people, whose needs they have categorised, into an existing system of provision based on 'funding matrices' which are specific to each authority (DfEE 1996), despite the Code specifying that 'a child has special educational needs if he or she has a learning difficulty which calls for special educational provision to be made for him or her' (DfE 1994, 2.1, p.5). How do parents attempt to 'transfer the power' (Booth 1988) and challenge LEA decisions?

A case study: Michael

Michael, aged seven, lives in a shire LEA although his school is in the catchment area of a New Town which has rural villages on its outskirts. This LEA has a funding regime which allocates £2,300 to a pupil categorised as having moderate learning difficulties and requiring support in mainstream.

Michael initially received support from this arrangement. However, at his annual review meeting, his parents and the headteacher recognised that he should continue to receive 20 hours support from a learning support assistant, but that the £2,300 would not cover this level of support for the year. Consequently the parents asked the LEA to specify the 20 hours support from a learning support assistant on Michael's statement so that the LEA would provide the extra resources. A meeting was held with the assistant education officer, a letter from this officer records the LEA's perspective:

> The LEA does not write into Statements of Special Educational Needs a specified number of hours. I do not recall any specific comment about the 20 hours welfare assistant support, except to make it clear that £2,300 was the level of support for pupils with moderate learning difficulties in mainstream schools. The AWPU and Statemented pupil allowance (approximately £150) should be added to this figure.

The parents decided to go to the Special Educational Needs Tribunal:

> We are appealing under Section 170 of the 1993 Education Act, against the provision set out in Michael's statement, on the grounds that the LEA has failed to specify as it should the provision which Michael should receive, in particular in the areas of classroom support and speech therapy.

While the parents were waiting for their appeal to be heard an annual review meeting was held to discuss Michael's progress and his imminent transfer from first school to middle school. Present at this meeting were the headteacher (Michael's class teacher), a speech and language therapist, an information technology specialist teacher, the assistant education officer, the educational psychologist and Michael's mother. His mother and father had asked me to attend as their 'friend' – whom they presumably trusted.

During this meeting, which lasted three hours, the assistant education officer for the LEA pointed out that the educational psychologist's report showed that Michael had an intelligence quotient of 57. He went on to point out that children with an IQ score of 50 or thereabouts should be in a school for children with severe learning difficulties. The educational psychologist told the education officer that 'under the old system' that may have applied.

I looked over at Claire, Michael's mother, who was close to tears and the meeting had only just begun. Claire is the Chairperson of the local Network '81 group – which is affiliated to a national network of parent-led support and information groups, set up after the 1981 Education Act. Here was Claire, a professional educator, the Chairperson of a local parents group she had set up, who was being confronted about her choice of mainstream education for her child. With Michael's father, she had ensured that Michael was removed from a special school for children with 'moderate learning difficulties' and that their choice of a mainstream school in their locality was on Part 4 of Michael's statement.

This annual review meeting was re-convened and the headteacher wrote the recommendations for the amended statement which were agreed by the educational psychologist and Claire. When the final statement was produced the parents' request for mainstream school had been disregarded and a unit for children with severe communication difficulties was on the statement. This unit was to be opened within six months. This statement would have to be appealed against at a different tribunal to where the failure to specify provision was to be heard. Fortunately for Michael, his parents were successful in their appeal, the LEA was ordered to amend the statement to include eighteen hours, eventually fulltime, of welfare assistant support. The chairperson of the tribunal wrote that:

> We are unable to accept that the LEA has discharged its obligation to identify provision which it considers necessary to meet Michael's needs by allocating a lump sum, without adequate guidance and oversight on how that funding is to be spent ... Part 3 of the statement should specify the amount and level of provision which Michael is to receive to meet all the needs identified in Part 2. In reaching this conclusion we have had regard to Part B of the Education (Special Educational Needs) Regulations 1994, paragraphs 4:24, 4:28, 4:29 of the Code of Practice and the decision in Ex parte E.

The special educational panel of this shire county has the tribunal decisions reported to them. These were registered as 'recent tribunal cases', which were confidential. However, it was recorded at this meeting that the members of the panel, who are elected councillors, were concerned about the financial implications of the tribunal and that these should be registered with the Chief Executive and the legal position should be sought. In the same records of this meeting the funding position for pupils categorised as having moderate learning difficulties who receive support in mainstream (this also includes pupils with specific learning difficulties in this category) was underspent by £130,000. Claire, and two other mothers who belong to their local Network '81 group, have also been successful in their tribunals. Two of these parents have decided to take their cases to the local authority ombudsman on the grounds of maladministration leading to injustice.

Claire and her partner challenged the LEA and went to the SEN Tribunal to ensure the provision they perceived their child was entitled to. They went through a process of empowerment, they sought information and advice from organisations such as the Independent Panel for Special Education Advice, they set up a parents group to decrease their isolation and to support other parents who were going through similar difficulties.

The growth of parent organisations

Since the 1981 Education Act a number of parent groups have arisen to campaign in the area of special education (Wolfendale 1989). This legislation has provided an impetus to the emergence of parent groups because individually parents have found it difficult to understand and to be able to get the special educational provision that they want for their child. Parents have set up localised and national groups, some of which network together. These parent groups campaign over specific issues such as the right of children to be included into mainstream schools with adequate resources. The 'pro-integration' groups support and give parents advice on how to secure the provision that they want for their child, be it mainstream or special schooling.

Gathering parents' perspectives

The growth of parent organisations which have been set up in England since the implementation of the 1981 Education Act in 1983 will be discussed by considering the views of parents who have innovated or been involved in these groups. I wanted to find out about the experiences of the individual parents who were a part of these groups and to gather information about how the parent group's functioned. Eight parents were interviewed who have been involved in the campaign and support groups Network '81 (Arrondelle 1990), Liaison for those involved in the needs of children, Campaign for Choice, Parents in Partnership, and Supportive Parents for Special Children (Broomhead and Darley 1992). The views and experiences of the parents involved in four groups – Parents in Partnership, Integration Alliance (now the Alliance for Inclusive Education), Network '81 and Campaign for Choice will be presented. Their perspectives indicate how their experiences have led to their involvement in campaign and support groups in the area of special education.

Parents in Partnership and Integration Alliance

Diana, the parent support worker for Parents in Partnership described the London-based group which was set up in 1984 as: 'A parents' campaign for integrated education, post the '81 Act, a lobbying group'. Since the breakup of the Inner London Education Authority in 1989, Parents in Partnership includes all the inner and outer London boroughs. There is a telephone advice line available for parents to call for information and support about their children's education. While the group will provide support and advice for parents regardless of whether they want their child to be integrated into mainstream school, the group does focus on campaigning for integrated education. The reason for this was that the group found that 'the '81 Education Act caused a lot of difficulties for parents who want to make integration work'. Diana recognised that not all parents can 'fight' for integration. Some give up even though they want their children to be a part of mainstream schools: 'Parents are desperate for their children to be welcomed in the world and the people who have any energy left to do the fighting want to make the world more responsive for their child'.

Diana conceptualised the difficulties facing parents as a 'deficit view of disability in society', rather than a social model of disability which accepts all children and young people. According to Diana society creates inequality and prejudice against disability: 'What parents of children with "special needs" find is all the prejudice which anybody with a disability finds'. Diana's perspective is that parents need support to enable them to get beyond a 'deficit' view of disability. This is a part of the work of Parents in Partnership which Diana says is to: 'Take parents, wherever they happen to be in this range of experience and try to empower them on to the next bit'. Diana explained how she empowers parents:

> There's a range of things, accessibility on the telephone, people can phone us and get from us a range of information, just basic, what people's rights are, what the legislation actually means, whether the professionals or the people they are surrounded by are actually doing it according to the book. Then we can do a lot of listening, just a sort of counselling role, people get rid of some of the anger and disappointment that has built up, either just because of parenting a child with learning difficulties, or just because of the way they've been treated.

Parents in Partnership co-ordinates referrals from the same London borough and small groups of parents can then become pressure groups. She has been involved in setting up the national organisation 'Integration Alliance' (now the Alliance for Inclusive Education), a pro-integration campaign group, led by disabled people to which parents and educators are allied.

Micheline, a disabled parent, the Disability Equality Advisor to Parents in Partnership and a founder member of the Alliance for Inclusive Education has co-written a book on disability equality issues in the classroom (Rieser and Mason 1990). Micheline found that her daughter's first primary school required her to support the headteacher who took responsibility for the child, the training of staff, and employing the right helpers and was 'a good ally'. When her daughter's helper became 'over protective' Micheline had to go into school to make sure her child was able to be with her friends, as according to Micheline and her daughter, the helper was putting the other children off and was a negative adult influence around her. Micheline felt like a 'naughty' parent because she was not satisfied with the staff member whom the school thought was a 'wonderful person': 'I had the feeling that what I was doing was naughty, I was being naughty and that was why I had this "difficult" child'. She thought that her involvement in her child's schooling was 'inevitable' because her daughter is disabled: 'That was part of my commitment. You know, like I think I can't leave it up to my daughter, a little tot, to take on the able-bodied community'.

Micheline's daughter moved schools because of the lack of physical access around her first school. Micheline remained a governor at that school because she wants to carry on dispelling the staff's fears about disability and so that the staff 'can't accuse me of only looking after my own child's interest'. For Micheline, education is more than curriculum subjects.

It is 'much more to do with the way we learn who we are in the world and what your place is and what there is to be done'.

The perspectives of Micheline and Diana indicate how their involvement has developed through their experiences as parents of children who require support to access mainstream schooling. Diana considers how parents require support in order to understand 'the system' in which they are exposed to prejudicial attitudes due to the deficit view of disability in society. Parents in Partnership aims to enable parents to articulate what they want for their child's education and to co-ordinate a national strategy for inclusive education. In May 1996 Parents in Partnership changed to 'Parents for Inclusion' in order to recognise that 'true' partnership with professionals is not possible, as professionals have the power to exclude children against the wishes of parents and the child. Parents in Partnership state that they want to show a commitment to the disability movement in their fight for civil rights and campaign for inclusive education. At the same time, the group recognised in a letter to its members in May 1996 that:

> There are many parent members (including elected officers of the executive) who have had to accept separate specialist provision, because of this lack of real choice. This has not stopped them working for the principle that it is *the system* that must stop rejecting and failing children because of their differences.

Network '81

Elizabeth and David set up the national parents group Network '81 as a direct result of their experiences with their daughter. She had been at primary school for a year without 'additional back-up', at around the same time the 1981 Act had introduced the statementing process. While they had a lot of support they were concerned that many parents would be unable to understand that they could make a contribution to the statementing process. The statementing procedure had left a lasting impression on them:

> It was quite complicated and horrendous at that stage, it's something that you can never be prepared for. So the whole thing comes as a tremendous shock. You have to find out so much that you'd never even given a thought to before until you're into it up to here, without being prepared for it. And all parents are in the same situation, are involved in circumstances for which they are totally unprepared.
>
> (Elizabeth)

Elizabeth and David thought it was important that they understood the statementing procedure, but they were fearful and had to do a 'balancing act' which required them to present their case in the best way possible. They wanted to be able to contribute to the decision-making over their child's education and the only way to ensure that their child received resources – support in mainstream – was to go through the statementing process. They consider themselves 'lucky' to have heard Mark Vaughan (the founder of the Centre for Studies on Integrated Education (now Inclusive Education)) talking on the radio about statementing, and they then contacted him. Their experience made them aware of the position of other parents:

> Why we are here is that there is so little information disseminated to parents that we are here to help. Parents are suddenly confronted with pages and pages of legal jargon about their children with 'special needs'. It's very scary and very isolating. We found this. I mean, we started off in the same position. It was the 'professionals' and us, very, very isolating and unpleasant.
>
> (David)

By 1991, eight years after the implementation of the 1981 Education Act, the group had achieved charitable status and funding from Children in Need. At the time when Elizabeth and David were talking to me, the office of the parents' group was in their own sitting room where they answered telephone calls to support parents and give them advice. Elizabeth and David felt that they couldn't 'solve cases' but they can make suggestions and will refer people on to other organisations for advice and information. They saw their priority as arranging advocacy training sessions for parents and feel that they have achieved the 'dissemination of information' as well as having supported distraught parents. Network '81 also support the setting up of local parent lobbying groups such as the Milton Keynes group chaired by Michael's mother. Support in the form of financial assistance for hiring rooms to meet and postage advertising initial meetings are provided and the co-ordinator from the national group will speak at meetings. In 1996 Network '81 had 500 members and 67 local parent pressure groups affiliated to them, 30 of these are local Network '81 groups. Fifty-five trained advocacy befrienders provide individual help nationally to parents. The group also receive funding directly from the Department for Education and Employment for training on Parent Partnership information days with LEAs around the country. Training requested by LEAs for their Named person has also been carried out by the group which has expanded to include four part-time staff including administrators and a fundraiser who are involved in producing a quarterly newsletter. While the group does not campaign by 'waving banners' according to the national co-ordinator, the group encourages parents to go out and question how LEAs respond to their requests for the provision they want for their child. The group believes 'very much in inclusive education' and sets out to 'empower parents as to how to go about getting it in mainstream schools' according to the co-ordinator. The group does also try to help parents whose children are in special schools, who may feel that they have been 'let down' by mainstream schools.

Campaign for Choice

Paul was Chair of the parents group 'Campaign for Choice' which emerged in the late 1980s. This group met to campaign against the proposals of the ILEA's report chaired by John Fish (ILEA 1985), a committee of 25 met to lobby and carry out demonstrations against what they perceived to be the ILEA's proposals to close special schools.

> It was like a brush fire really. We organised ourselves in the school and then we started contacting other schools and gradually gathered together parents and suddenly there was this organisation and we were having meetings with three hundred parents.

Campaign for Choice were successful in their aims and the policy was modified to take into account the views of parents who wanted special schools maintained by the authority. Paul's main area of concern in special education is that integration should not happen 'on the cheap'. Paul hopes that the 'debate on integration' is 'turned on it's head' with money put into education 'so that integration is done properly and special schools are done properly'.

Parents' perspectives

The views and experiences of these parents were formed around the following themes: school choice and LEAs, statementing, integration, special schools, welcoming schools, conflict and collaboration with professionals (Paige-Smith 1996a). While these parents want different forms of education for their child, special or mainstream schools, they have a common concern about the position of their child in education and society. These parents have gone through a process of empowerment in order to represent their views and their political action has involved the empowerment of others through advice giving and the formation of local and national pressure and support groups.

Supporting all parents?

Local voluntary organisations such as the Elfrida Rathbone Society in Camden, London, has two advocates available to provide practical support, information and advice to parents on the education of their children with learning difficulties or disabilities. One of these advocates is funded by the LEA to provide independent advice for the Bengali community. The rest of the project receives funding from Children in Need. In 1996 they had 250 'active' cases of parents who were working towards self-empowerment. The advocates will write letters of parental representation towards the statementing process, and will accompany parents to meetings at school, at LEA offices as well as represent parents at SEN tribunals. The London-based Advisory Centre for Education is a voluntary organisation that was estabished in 1960 by a group of mothers living in Cambridge, who wanted to demystify the world of education, to encourage schools and institutions to recognise the importance of a good parent–school partnership (ACE 1991). In 1991 almost 50 per cent of their calls to their daily telephone advice line were in the area of special needs, the majority of these were concerned with parents' rights and information. The centre will support parent campaigns by providing information, advice on the telephone and may send a speaker on parents' rights to meetings (Paige-Smith 1996b). The British Dyslexia Association set up in 1972 by Marian Welchman, the mother of a dyslexic child, campaigns for provision for young people with 'specific learning difficulties' and most of the people involved in this lobbying group are either parents of dyslexic children or have dyslexia themselves. The aims of the group are that there should be proper teaching, help and support and equal opportunities for children and adults with dyslexia. The group has a network of befrienders in each LEA who provide emotional and educational advice and support to parents.

The Warnock Report (DES 1978) acknowledged that the growth of voluntary organisations, such as the Dyslexia Association, would focus on 'specialised areas of need' in terms of different disabilities (DES 1978, 17.9). The report also recognised that there was a lack of representation for young people categorised as having 'moderate learning difficulties' and 'emotional and behavioural problems' who were noted to be the largest group of children with special educational needs. While the parent groups such as Network '81, Parents in Partnership and voluntary organisations such as the Advisory Centre for Education set out to provide advice and support for all parents, and in the case of Elfrida Rathbone in Camden the group specifically supports the Bengali community, each organisation recognises that they can only reach those parents who approach them for support. The British Dyslexia Association can provide advice to have a child assessed by a psychologist for £200 and give advice on the assessment process, however, the group does not provide funding for many parents who may not be able to afford to pay for this private assessment. Network '81 consider their job as trying to reach the parents who are not empowered who 'pack it all in' as well as supporting empowered parents to get the provision they perceive their child is entitled to.

A study by Gross recognises that 'the trend amongst pupils with emotional and behavioural difficulties is one of increasing segregation' (Gross 1996, p.7), suggesting that perhaps the parents of these children do not access their rights to prevent their exclusion into special schools. Tomlinson (1986) in her study of the social construction of children with moderate learning difficulties asserted that middle-class parents are more likely to oppose the exclusion of their child to a stigmatised form of schooling. Gross considers this link between parental advocacy and the securing of resource allocation for integration especially for the '"middle class" special needs such as Down's Syndrome, Specific Learning Difficulties, language disorder, sensory impairment, physical disability' (Gross 1996, p.4). Parent choice and parent involvement in the market place of competition for resources which are a part of the LEAs special education budget may have shifted towards a 'rights' model of accessing resources which favours middle-class, articulate parents. However, parents have few 'rights' to exercise in comparison to the decision-making powers of LEAs under the 1993 Education Act.

In Ontario, Canada, 'Bill '82', the Education Amendment Act, 1980, is similar to the legislation in this country in so far as special education should be suited to the needs and abilities of the child making school authorities legally accountable for what is done to and for the child in school (Dickinson and Mackay 1989). This has been considered to be a 'major invasion of the rights of working class parents and students to obtain equality of educational opportunity in Ontario' because there is a disproportionate representation of children of lower socio-economic status in special educational programmes (Dickinson and Mackay 1989, p.218). Two reasons for this are identified – certain pupils are more likely to be segregated into special education programmes and their parents are less likely to be involved in ensuring integration.

In Canada there is an established network of 400 local parent groups which are a part of the national parents group the Canadian Association of Community Living (CACL) which has a commitment to supporting parents in their demands for inclusive education. Initially this group was set up in the 1950s when parents began counselling other parents, became known as 'community resource parents' and formed the Canadian Association for the Mental Retarded which included family members, people with learning difficulties, professionals and interested citizens (Dybwad 1983). Their priority was to create alternatives to the institutionalisation of their children and established classes and eventually schools for their children who were at that time denied access to public schools. The Canadian constitution also includes the 1981 Charter of Rights and Freedoms, and this legislation on equality rights provision has been used by parents to demand their children's rights to inclusion in education (McCallum 1991).

The Canadian parents' organisations, which come under the umbrella group of the CACL, have a long link with disabled people being involved. In England the Alliance for Inclusive Education could be considered to be a similar organisation, involving parents, professionals, interested citizens, disabled adults and young people. However, the issue of involving and empowering those parents who may not be able to access a system of voluntary organisations or take action once they are informed about their rights, remains in both countries. The parents who have become involved in parent groups act as advocates for their children, and provide support for other parents as well as attempting to generalise their experiences through networking with other parents on a local or national level. Some of these parents of children who have learning difficulties or disabilities may be professionals themselves. Holding information may not necessarily make their position more powerful if they are in the 'parent role' of a partnership relationship.

The growth of parent groups in England has occurred alongside the development of the 1980s education policies which promote a 'rights' model of parent participation. The impact of the parental lobby including voluntary groups has been to raise the profile of parent action on to a political level which includes directly challenging decision-making surrounding the education of children with learning difficulties or disabilities. This may take place in the courts (Rabinowicz 1992), at the Special Educational Needs Tribunal, through disability equality training, working with schools, lobbying at local and national levels and providing support and advice to parents.

In July 1996 at an international conference on Inclusive Education in Manchester, two parents from a Sheffield-based parent' group 'Parents with Attitude' recited two extracts from their book 'Let Our Children Be' (Murray and Renman 1996) as a part of the opening speeches. The emotional cost to families who attempt to change and challenge the school system around disability equality issues for young people who experience difficulties in learning or have disabilities is unmeasurable. Increasingly, parents are attempting to redefine the concept of 'partnership' with professionals in a way that recognises the expertise of parents as decision-makers through their involvement in their child's schooling. Increased collaboration between schools and parents, which acknowledges equality of opportunity for young people with learning difficulties or disabilities through access to: school buildings, the curriculum and learning support, could begin to dissipate the search for justice through confrontation.

References

ACE (1991) *Information Sheet.* London: ACE.

Arrondelle, E. (1990) 'Kirsty: the struggle for a place in ordinary school' in Rieser, R. and Mason, M. (Eds) *Disability Equality in the Classroom: a human rights issue.* London: Inner London Education Authority.

Booth, T. (1988) 'Challenging Conceptions of Integration' in Barton (Ed.) *The Politics of Special Educational Needs.* Sussex: Falmer Press.

Broomhead, R. and Darley, P. (1992) 'Supportive Parents for Special Children: working toward partnership in Avon' (Eds) Booth, T. *et al. Policies for Diversity in Education.* London: Routledge.

Centre for Studies on Inclusive Education, 1 Redland Close, Elm Lane, Redland, Bristol, BS6 6UE.

Cornwell, N. (1987) *Statementing and the 1981 Education Act.* Bedford: Cranfield Press.

Department of Education and Science (1978) *Special Educational Needs* (The Warnock Report). London: HMSO.

Department of Education and Science (1981) *The Education Act.* London: HMSO.

Department For Education (1993) *The Education Act,* Ch. 35. London: HMSO.

Department For Education (1994) *Code of Practice on the Identification and Assessment of Special Educational Needs,* October. London: HMSO.

Department For Education and Employment (1996) Circular SENCL 1/96, March 1996.

Dickinson, G. and Mackay, A. (1989) *Rights Freedoms and the Education System in Canada: cases and materials.* Toronto: Emond, Montgomery Publications.

Dybwad, G. (1983) 'The Achievement of Parent Organisations' Mullick, J. and Siegfried, M. (Eds) *Parent–Professional Partnerships in Developmental Disability Services.* Cambridge, Mass: The Ware Press.

Gross, J. (1996) 'The Weight of the Evidence: parental advocacy and resource allocation to children with statements of special educational need', *Support for Learning,* 11, 1, pp.3–8.

House of Commons Education Committee (1996) *Special Educational Needs; the working of the Code of Practice and the Tribunal,* Education Committee. London: HMSO.

The Independent Panel for Special Education Advice, 4 Ancient House Mews, Woodbridge, Suffolk, IP12 1DH.

Inner London Education Authority (1985) *Educational Opportunities for All?* Research Studies. London: ILEA.

McCallum, D. (1991) 'Access to Equality in Education: the power of parents' in Porter, L. and Richler, D. (Eds) *Changing Canadian Schools.* Ontario The Roeher Institute.

Murray, P. and Renman, J. (1996) *Let Our Children Be.* Sheffield: Parents With Attitude.

Network '81, 1–7 Woodfield Terrace, Stanstead, Essex, CM24 8AJ.

Paige-Smith, A. (1996a) 'Choosing to Campaign – a case study of parent choice, statementing and integration', *European Journal of Special Needs Education.* London: Routledge.

Paige-Smith, A. (1996b) 'Seeing Off Cuts – a parent and professional campaign to save inclusive education in a London Borough' in O'Hanlon (Ed.) *Professional Development Through Action Research in Educational Settings.* London: Falmer Press.

Rabinowicz, J. (1992) 'Children, Special Needs and the Courts', *British Journal of Special Education,* 19, 4, p.131.

Rieser, R. and Mason, M. (1990) *Disability Equality in the Classroom: a human rights issue.* London: Inner London Education Authority.

Russell, P. (1994) 'The Code of Practice: new partnerships for children with special educational needs', *British Journal of Special Education,* 21, pp.48–52.

Tomlinson, S. (1986) 'The Social Construction of the ESN(m) Child' in Cohen, A. and Cohen, L. (Eds) *Special Educational Needs in the Ordinary School.* London: Harper and Row.

Wolfendale, S. (1989) 'Parental Involvement and Power-sharing in Special Needs', in Wolfendale, S. (Ed.) *Parental Involvement.* London: Cassell Educational.

5 Implementing partnership with parents in schools

Sally Beveridge

The purpose of this chapter is to explore the ways in which schools are developing their relationships with parents. It presents perspectives on current school practice which are derived from interviews carried out by the author with a small number of parents of children with special educational needs and the Special Educational Needs Co-ordinators (SENCOs) of the schools their children attend. It sets these against a preliminary consideration of the potential contribution that parents have to make in assessment, decision-making and review, in order to identify ways in which schools might continue to develop and extend their approach in line with the Code of Practice (DfE 1994a).

The Code of Practice describes partnership between professionals and parents as one of the 'fundamental principles' which should underpin assessment, decision-making and review procedures. In doing so, it reasserts the argument which was put unequivocally by the Warnock Committee (DES 1978), that the involvement of parents as partners in the educational process is essential for the successful education of children with special educational needs.

Schools and teachers have on the whole become aware that they need to try to promote positive home–school liaison. Since the publication of the Warnock Report, they have been left in no doubt by the educational legislation of the 1980s and 1990s that parents have important rights in relation to their children's formal education. Rights for all parents, summarised in the Parent's Charter (DfE 1994b), include access to information about their own child's progress and attainments as well as about whole-school policies and practices. For those parents whose children have a statement of special educational need, further rights include involvement in the initial statutory assessment procedures and in subsequent annual reviews. At the same time as legislative changes have formalised parents' rights, educational research has identified good communication between home and school as a significant factor which is associated with effective schools (Mortimore *et al.* 1988, Reynolds and Cuttance 1992). There has also been increasing evidence of the benefits for children's learning when their teachers and parents have been able to collaborate actively together, for example on the teaching of reading (e.g. Wolfendale and Topping 1996). On both legislative and educational grounds, therefore, many schools explicitly acknowledge the importance of constructive relationships with parents.

The Warnock Report and the Code of Practice use the term 'partnership' to describe the nature of the relationship which teachers should seek to develop with parents. The term is frequently used by teachers and other professionals to describe a range of different forms of collaboration. However, partnership is not so much a characteristic of a particular form of home–school contact as of the *quality of the interaction* which takes place. The concept of partnership is based on the recognition that parents and teachers have complementary contributions to make to children's education. Accordingly, it is central to the notion of partnership that schools should demonstrate that they not only listen to, but also value, parents' perspectives. Many teachers aim to do this, but it must be acknowledged that the parental experience of contact with school can be far removed from the partnership ideal. The following extract from one of the author's interviews, with a mother of an eleven year-old son (on Stage One of the Code of Practice assessment procedures), gives a flavour of the apprehensions and pressures that parents can feel, as well as their perceptions of unfounded assumptions. Asked to say what advice she would give to other parents about communication with school, she replied:

> As a parent, you've got to get involved ... You may feel intimidated but you must put your own self to one side, not be intimidated, and say 'this is what I feel, I think, I wish for my child', and be ready to say 'you're making assumptions – look, you're wrong'. Sometimes teachers are so harassed and pressurised and stressed that to say they've got to reach out to parents may be too much. But as a parent you do feel the barriers are there, you feel pressurised to justify yourself a lot – there needs to be a way to bring the barriers down.

This, far from unique, perspective illustrates that there is plenty of scope for schools to continue to review their parent–teacher relationships. In theory, it can be argued that the introduction of the Code of Practice has provided them with the impetus to do so (Beveridge 1995).

The framework provided by the Code of Practice

The Code of Practice describes communication with parents as central to school policy for meeting special educational needs. For constructive communication to take place, schools need to consider the information they provide, their accessibility and their arrangements for promoting working partnerships with parents. Taking each of these in turn, firstly, parents must be provided with clear and accurate information about the school's SEN policy, the support which will be available for their child and the ways in which they can expect to be consulted and involved in the educational process. Secondly, schools should look at ways of making themselves as approachable as possible, so that the information they provide is accessible and readily understood, and that parents feel neither inhibited nor anxious about making contact with staff. Thirdly, there need to be procedures in place for encouraging, recording and responding to parental views, so that the provision schools make for children with special educational needs is fully informed by ongoing dialogue with their parents.

In the past, although practice has varied, when schools have involved parents it has been primarily:

- in the identification and preliminary assessment of children's needs;
- in specific interventions, where for example parents have been asked to support school by implementing programmes such as in reading or behaviour management at home;
- in the review of progress, for example through parent–teacher consultations, written reporting and, for parents of children with statements, through annual review procedures.

The Code of Practice introduces additional demands for schools which are of two main kinds. The first concerns the scope of the formalised procedures for involvement that it sets out. These emphasise the involvement of *all* parents of children with special educational needs, not only those whose children have statements; and they describe involvement throughout an *ongoing cycle* of assessment, decision-making and review. The second concerns the quality of the communication which is required. If the educational provision they make is to be properly informed by *two-way dialogue* with parents, then schools need to develop approaches which will both elicit and support parental contributions.

The parental contribution to assessment, decision-making and review

In their day-to-day family interactions, parents are in a position to observe, monitor and evaluate their children's development. It is not surprising therefore that they are often the first to identify any difficulties that their children experience. The Code of Practice recognises the role they can play in the early identification of special educational needs and argues that schools must be 'open and responsive to expressions of concern and information provided by parents' (DfE 1994a, para 2:17). The contribution that parents can make to assessment goes well beyond initial identification though. They have in-depth knowledge, information and experiences of their own children which are complementary to the wider curricular expertise and understanding of teaching and learning which teachers bring to the assessment process. Accordingly, parents can add a great deal to a teacher's understanding of their child's individual educational needs.

Wolfendale (1992) has reviewed the evidence from schemes which have sought to involve parents actively in the assessment and review of their children's progress. She summarises the picture which emerges of the potential parental contribution as follows:

- Parents have expertise in commenting on development.
- Parents' intimate knowledge of their children can be described by them.
- Parental information can complement professional information.
- The information can show up differing behaviour in different settings.
- The information can serve to highlight concerns regarding progress.
- Parents can provide a realistic appraisal of their children.

(p.80)

There is rather less evidence about the nature of parental contributions to decision-making. However, the Code of Practice is explicit that 'school-based action should take account of the wishes, feelings and knowledge of parents at all stages (DfE 1994a, para. 2:28). Parents have their own priorities for their children and insights into the sorts of strategies which might best meet their needs. It can be argued, therefore, that decision-making in school is likely to be more effective when teachers seek to acknowledge and incorporate parental perspectives.

Parents of children with statements have, of course, been involved at some level in assessment, decision-making and review procedures since the implementation of the 1981 Education Act. It is important to reflect upon what has been learned from their experience which has relevance for the extension of school practice across the wider range of special educational needs. Formal assessment can be stressful for parents, who are likely to wish for a full investigation of their child's difficulties but at the same time feel ambivalent about the possible outcomes. They can be distressed by the degree of emphasis placed on their child's weaknesses (Russell 1991) or, in some cases, on their own parenting skills (Galloway *et al.* 1994). The assessment of special educational need is a complex process which must take account of the interactive learning contexts in which difficulties arise. One result of this complexity, as Galloway and his colleagues found in their research (1994), is that there is real scope for misunderstanding and discrepancy in home and school perspectives. Further, while parents may feel confident in describing and reporting their perspectives on their children's behaviour during informal consultations, there is ample evidence that they may require structure and support to help them prepare their contributions for more formal assessment and review procedures (e.g. Wolfendale 1988, 1993, Hughes and Carpenter 1991). In the absence of such assistance, it is rare for parents to feel that their views have been taken fully into account. The feelings of powerlessness which can result may not be recognised by the teachers involved, because parents and professionals can come away from a meeting with very different perceptions of the role the parent has played in any decision-making which took place (Armstrong 1995).

If schools are to aim for genuine partnership with parents in assessment, decision-making and review, therefore, it would appear that teachers need to:

- recognise the personal and emotional investment of parents;
- focus on their children's strengths as well as weaknesses;

- refrain from making assumptions about the learning context of home;
- support parents in the preparation of their contributions;
- respect the validity of differing perspectives, or the 'legitimacy of dissent' (Dale 1996);
- seek constructive ways of reconciling different viewpoints.

Parent and teacher perspectives on current school practice

Interviews were carried out with parents and teachers in the spring term of 1996, that is, during the second school year following publication of the Code of Practice. The focus was on their perspectives concerning parental involvement in assessment, decision-making and review. The parents were interviewed individually in their own homes. Their children, who attend both primary and secondary schools, all have special educational needs. Most do not have statements, but are on the school-based stages of assessment outlined in the Code of Practice.

Parental involvement in assessment

Not all of the parents felt that they had things to contribute to the assessment of their children's needs, although those who reported that they had been encouraged to participate by the school expressed satisfaction with their involvement. It should be noted that much of the following parental comment about initial identification and assessment refers to experiences in their child's previous, rather than current, school. Their current SENCOs were all explicit in interview about the potential role that parents could play in assessment, particularly during the early primary years and at transfer to secondary school. They described the ways in which parental knowledge can help inform the approach taken with their children. One who has extensive experience of working with parents in assessment described it as 'a learning process for us and for the parents as well'.

Most parents had been aware of the school's initial assessment of their childrens special educational needs, although this was not always clearly communicated. One mother reported: 'I wasn't always in the know. Things probably went on for about two years before I properly knew there was a real problem'. Another explained that she had known her son was having additional help with reading at school, and she had been involved by the school in tasks to do at home. However, she had not appreciated the extent of the school's concern, because she had had no discussion with the special needs staff about his progress, and at parent consultation evenings the class teachers 'just kept reassuring me every year'. It was only in the last year of primary school that she discovered how many difficulties her son was experiencing, when she was left 'feeling an inch high' by a teacher who, in her view, had only negative things to report.

For some parents there had been a significant discrepancy between their own perspectives and those of the school concerning the nature of their child's needs. In one case, school had communicated to the mother that her daughter's difficulties were to do with lack of effort: 'they thought she wouldn't rather than she couldn't'. It was only through first involvement with a professional from outside school, and later, on transfer to secondary school, that this mother felt her daughter's needs had been properly assessed by people who 'see her strengths as well as her weaknesses'. In a further example, a foster mother felt both distressed and frustrated that, from her perspective, her foster son's needs were being underestimated:

> The psychologist said there was nothing wrong with Paul. The teacher said Paul would work at school and the only problem was his homework. But the problem is not only his homework – he just wants to sit down and watch TV, eat, lie on his bed. To get washed is a problem, everything is an effort for him.

The third instance is rather different, in that, from the parental perspective, staff had made so much of their daughter's shyness that they had created unnecessary difficulties for her at school: 'they were putting the light too much on Sophie'. The parents feel that their daughter's needs are handled more sensitively at secondary school, where home and school perspectives have been reconciled.

What links all three examples, is that the parents involved believed that professionals were attributing their children's difficulties at least in part to the home context, and were not listening to their point of view. The first felt strongly that the staff 'made out I didn't care and I didn't help – how dare they? I care more than they realise'. For the second: 'Parents know what their child is like and what their child is capable of ... they [professionals] don't seem to listen.' The third mother said that the staff had not sought her views, and further, 'I'm not sure they would have taken any notice of me ... Sophie didn't ever act at home like she did at school – that wasn't the real Sophie'.

In several cases, parents had already been aware that their child was experiencing some sort of difficulty before it was raised by school. One mother explained that she had not said anything throughout her daughter's primary schooling because: 'You think teachers know more than you and they'll pick up on it [if there is a difficulty]'. She went on to describe in vivid detail the dilemma she had experienced about whether she should approach the staff with her concerns:

> I had had doubts – was I making something out of nothing? Was I being a panicky mother? I wanted to be sure I wasn't jumping to conclusions and I held back for a while. I didn't want to make Claire think that there was a problem if there wasn't one. I didn't want to make too much of it ... now I wish that perhaps I'd done something sooner – but you can't win on that one. I would have felt dreadful going up to school to say 'I'm sure there's something wrong but I don't know what' – it looks as if you're overreacting.

Another mother discussed the ways in which the label of special educational needs could be stigmatising, for parents as well as their child, and she described the tension she felt between accepting her son as he was and wanting the best for him. Like most of the parents interviewed though, she was convinced that where children had particular needs, it was important that these should be identified as early as possible at school, so that appropriate help could be given. Further, all the parents were strongly of the view that if teachers had any concerns about their children, they wanted to know of these straight away.

Parental involvement in decision-making

There was no real consensus among the SENCOs about the extent to which parents might contribute to decision-making. Some drew a distinction between the informal and formal curriculum. That is, they expected that parents would participate in decisions about issues related to behaviour management and social interaction, but: 'on the academic side, I think they look to you [the teacher] for the help, to lead them ... they look to you for where to go next'. One secondary school SENCO said that ideally he would like parents to feel more involved, so that their views and priorities, 'how they see provision – what they want for their child', can inform the educational decisions that are made.

All believed that parents need to be kept in touch as fully as possible with decisions about provision for their children, and it is notable that one secondary school's SEN policy makes explicit the importance of building up parental trust:

> The success or otherwise of SEN provision in a school, as far as parents are concerned, is one of trust. Do they believe that the school, given all the constraints placed on it, is endeavouring to deliver a quality education for their child?

In reflecting upon the practice of their children's current schools, most parents demonstrated that they did indeed trust that staff were trying to do as much as possible for their children. Most were informed, at least at a general level, of the sort of help that their children were being given. Only one, however, made any reference to active participation in decision-making about provision. She described the way in which she had been involved in a discussion about what strategies might best meet her daughter's needs. She had been particularly impressed by the extent to which the SENCO had taken her daughter's feelings into consideration. A number of other parents also referred with approval to the way in which their children had been consulted about the nature of the support they might prefer.

Although parents may rarely have been active participants in decision-making, they were frequently asked by their children's schools to undertake specific tasks at home to support their children's learning. Of those parents whose children were at primary school, all reported some level of involvement of this kind which they either carried out themselves, or arranged for another family member or friend to do so. Among the parents whose children attended secondary school, fewer were engaged in giving this sort of assistance, and most described ways in which the forms of support they gave were changing as their children grew older. A commonly expressed aim was to make their children feel confident that they could be more independent and like their peers in the school work they completed at home.

Not all of the parents felt able to work directly with their children. For example, one mother said, 'he hasn't enough concentration to do it with me, he messes about too much, so Daddy does it'. Another described how, although she wanted to help her daughter, it was counterproductive if they tried to work on school tasks together, because they quickly became frustrated with one another. She felt under pressure as a result of what she perceived to be the reaction of others: 'It gets you down when you want to help her and you can't ... it's upsetting when people think I'm not helping her'.

Pressure was not only experienced by parents who were unable to work directly with their children. Two other mothers said they felt that primary school staff thought they should be doing more at home with their children, while one father was spending an hour each evening with his son on literacy tasks. By contrast, a foster mother had felt sufficiently confident to explain to the school that she thought it was too much for her young son to work on school tasks at home during the week, and she had come to an arrangement whereby activities were planned which could be tackled together at the weekends and during school holidays. The potential risks of adding to pressure on parents by asking them to work with their children at home were acknowledged by a primary school SENCO when she said:

> sometimes I get the feeling that parents think helping their children must take a long time every evening. I think they need to realise that helping can be five minutes every evening ... and not make it too onerous for them or the child ... We need to come to an understanding of what we expect of one another I think.

Parental involvement in the review of progress

Most parents described parent–teacher consultation evenings as their main means of communication with schools about their children's progress. In addition, nearly all indicated that they could initiate discussion with school staff if they felt the need to do so, and some had arrangements for contact with their children's teachers on a more regular basis.

In between any planned meetings with staff, parents had their own ways of judging their children's progress, for example, by checking their homework and drawing comparisons with other children ('though I know you shouldn't really compare'), and by monitoring their general emotional well-being. Some parents were appreciative of being kept informed by school on a regular basis about their children's positive achievements as well as about any concerns, whereas others suggested that they were happy when they had no contact because they felt 'no news is good news'. All, however, were explicit that they would wish to know straight away if their children's progress were slower or poorer than expected, 'because the longer you leave it lapsed the worse it gets', and several felt they needed a more regular channel of communication. For example:

- 'if there's a problem, I'd want to know ... I suppose now and again it would be nice to know that she's getting on OK, which I don't. It would be reassuring to know ...'
- 'Ben's independence is important to him and I don't want to show him up, make him look different ... [but] you only get to see the teachers on parents' consultation evenings. I think if you have a child like Ben you need more.'

Outside the context of the twice yearly parent–teacher consultation evenings, there was little evidence from the parents whose children were on the early stages of the Code of Practice that they had been involved in regular reviews. This corresponds with the views expressed by two SENCOs:

- 'I cannot believe that every time you do a review of an IEP [Individual Education Plan], every half term, that parents would wish [to participate] ... I don't think the parents would have time or would want to be involved on that basis';
- 'its a question with parents at Stage 1 and Stage 2 reviews – how much do they really want to be involved? Do they want letters saying "can you come up to school for a review meeting", only to be told that their child is progressing very well, doing OK?'.

These may well be accurate perceptions about the availability of many parents and of their readiness to attend frequent formal reviews. However, a number of alternative forms of communication, including use of a home–school book or the telephone, were suggested by those parents who expressed a wish for more information and consultation about progress.

When parents had been asked to attend formal reviews, they had not always been fully prepared for the nature and purpose of the meeting. In one example, a mother had not been aware that the meeting had been called to review the school's concerns about her son's behaviour:

> I walked into that meeting not knowing – just thinking it was going to be a small discussion ... if there's problems, they should tell you, because you know, parents can help. It's no good not saying anything and leaving it till it's getting out of hand and calling big meetings and jumping down our throats ... I'm sat there saying, 'Well, I didn't know', and you know, I thought, 'They don't believe me' ... I could have prepared you know, had some evidence to put forward to show what I mean about what happens at home ... unprepared, you're just on the defensive all the time.

One secondary school had developed a model in its annual reviews for children with statements, whereby parents are first involved in informal pre-review discussions with the SENCO about the meeting's agenda. They are then encouraged to put their perspectives in writing to bring to the formal meeting. Formal meetings can always be inhibiting for parents, who may feel: 'you don't seem to say what you want to say – you feel very tense, it's not as relaxed as it should be'. Had this sort of approach been followed with the mother in the example above, however, she should have been clearer about the purposes of the meeting she was to attend, and might have participated in decisions about the agenda for discussion. She could also have prepared her own contribution in the same way that the staff had done, and would have been less likely to feel defensive and put on the spot.

Developing and extending practice

Parents and teachers shared some common perspectives about ways forward for developing and extending school practice by building on current strengths. Key factors appear to be:

- approachability;
- genuine care and concern;
- channels for two-way communication.

Approachability

Teachers described the importance of being open, available, making parents feel comfortable and always responding to their initiations. One explained: 'I want parents to feel OK about coming in and I do a lot of work to try to encourage them to do that'. The parents responded positively to this approach, for example:

- 'you don't feel hesitant, you can talk to her';
- 'he's very approachable, you can relax with him';
- 'they make time for you, which makes you feel better';
- 'at first you think, should I mention this, should I mention that, but once you've talked to them they tend to put you at your ease ... they give you the impression that it's all right, you can talk'.

Genuine care and concern

Parents attached a great deal of importance to the way in which teachers demonstrated awareness and sensitivity to their children's needs, and genuine care and concern about their progress. They also appreciated the ways in which some teachers attempted to involve their children in decisions about the support they might receive. One mother expressed feelings which were shared by a number of parents when she said: '[The SENCO] really does care. If you care and you've got a teacher like that, then your relationship's made'.

From the teachers' perspective, a shared concern for the child plays a significant role in the development of mutual respect:

> we've got to work closely together – there are some crucial issues to respond to – there are always differences of opinion, and we've got to have a mutual respect for each other, for each other's perception and point of view, and for where were actually coming from in terms of the student.

Channels of two-way communication

One SENCO described his need for open channels of communication with parents as follows:

> I'm reliant on the parents very often – if something's happened at school I want to be able to say to them 'I'm not very happy about this, can you fill me in?' I want to be able to talk to them at that level.

Parents expressed similarly clear views on two-way communication, for example: 'I can really talk with [the SENCO] because he doesn't brush it off ... I've no problems there – if I have a problem, it gets talked about, it doesn't get brushed under the carpet'. They saw communication as fundamental to building up relationships with their children's teachers:

- 'teachers could be more forward and tell you their concerns';
- 'parents need to talk to teachers more and know what children are doing at school – getting to know teachers and them getting to know you is important';
- 'it's important that teachers listen';
- 'it's teamwork – I don't think teachers can do it all alone';
- 'anything that builds relationships and communication has to be a good idea'.

In order to build on current strengths in schools, as a number of parents pointed out, it is not enough for the SENCOs to be committed to communication with parents. Rather, there is a need for an approach in which the staff as a whole demonstrate their openness and willingness to listen, and the value they place on parental insights and contributions to their children's learning. This means that whole-school policies should be developed in ways which support close home–school liaison, and staff development practices should promote the positive attitudes, skills, knowledge and understanding that teachers need if they are to work constructively with parents (Beveridge 1996).

Since the introduction of the Code of Practice, an understandable priority for many schools has been the development of within-school systems for assessment, decision-making and review, and some have barely begun to consider the involvement of parents in these. For other schools, particularly those with a well-established commitment to promoting positive home–school relationships, the impact of the Code has primarily been to make their procedures more systematic, and their contacts with parents more focused. There is no doubt that some of the expectations of the Code, especially those which concern parental involvement in the earliest school-based stages of assessment, pose major practical difficulties of resourcing, particularly in large secondary schools. As one SENCO acknowledged:

> short cuts are made, and I dare say for most high schools they will be made at Stage 2 or at Stages 1 and 2 ... While school is aware of its responsibilities to students at Stage 2, we're not able to fulfil these as well as we'd want to.

Continuing challenges

In addition to practical difficulties such as those just outlined, schools also face further continuing challenges if they are to extend their work with parents in line with the Code of Practice. These challenges fall into two main areas concerned with:

- clarity and style of communication;
- eliciting parental contributions.

Clarity and style of communication

Since August 1995, all schools have been required by law to have a written SEN policy, and they should make this accessible to parents. However, there was little evidence from the parents' interviews that they were familiar with the school SEN policy or with their children's IEPs. This does not necessarily imply that the schools had made no attempt to provide parents with this information. It does suggest though that there is a need to look closely at the way relevant information is communicated.

There certainly appears to be scope for schools to share documentation more readily with parents, and to supplement spoken communication with written information. For example, one school was considering developing leaflets for parents, including both common information on the framework of staged assessment and review, and also information more specific to their children's needs. Staff in this school recognised that they should seek to consult with parents about what they wanted to know, as well as to enlist their help in making the information as specific and readily understandable as possible. Another SENCO described the work that staff in his school had put into the development of report writing, with the aim of finding a balance between providing sufficient information without overwhelming parents

There is also scope for schools to extend the range of ways in which they keep parents in touch with their children's progress. While a number of parents said that they kept their fingers crossed that 'no news was good news', they expressed real appreciation of those teachers who provided frequent information about their children's positive achievements and progress as well as about any concerns. Some had a regular arrangement to call in to see the teacher at school, some used the telephone and others would prefer the information to be in written form, with the opportunity to think about and add their views to what was said: 'just three lines would do, just to say how they're getting on, if they're doing all right or if there are any problems'.

Eliciting parental contributions

Parents are not always aware of the potential contributions that they have to make to assessment, decision-making and review, and therefore schools need to explore ways of:

- helping parents see what they might contribute;
- providing opportunities for their contributions;
- providing encouragement and support, where appropriate, for their contributions.

While both parents and teachers tend to express a preference for more relaxed and informal meetings, there may be differing perceptions of what constitutes informality. It is essential that schools provide adequate information for parents about the nature and purpose of any meeting, and enable parents to be properly prepared for their participation.

Parents rarely feel confident in their knowledge of the formal academic curriculum, and may well expect teachers to take the lead in decisions about appropriate interventions for their children. Nevertheless, they have perspectives and priorities which should be addressed. This is particularly important in those situations where they are being asked to support school interventions through engaging in specific tasks with their child at home. Parents are less likely to feel pressurised if they have contributed to decisions about the form such support will take, taking into account, for example, the family routines and activities which contribute to the learning context of home.

There is no doubt that parent and professional perspectives can differ, and if significant discrepancies in interpretations of a child's needs persist, professional views tend to dominate in a way which can add greatly to family stress. Teachers need to continue to develop their skills of listening to what parents say, accepting the validity of differing viewpoints and finding ways of reconciling these wherever possible. It is only through extending their practice in these ways that the full benefits of partnership with parents in assessment, decision-making and review are likely to be seen.

References

Armstrong, D. (1995) *Power and Partnership in Education.* London: Routledge.

Beveridge, S. (1995) 'Patterns of Partnership' *Special*, 4, 3, pp.15–17.

Beveridge, S. (1996) *Spotlight on Special Educational Needs: learning difficulties.* Tamworth: NASEN.

Dale, N. (1996) *Working With Families of Children With Special Needs.* London: Routledge.

DES (1978) *Special Educational Needs* (The Warnock Report). Cmnd 7212. London: HMSO.

DfE (1994a) *Code of Practice on the Identification and Assessment of Special Educational Needs.* London: HMSO.

DfE (1994b) *Our Children's Education: the updated Parents' Charter.* London: HMSO.

Galloway, D., Armstrong, D. and Tomlinson, S. (1994) *The Assessment of Special Educational Needs: whose problem?* London: Longman.

Hughes, N. and Carpenter, B. (1991) 'Annual Reviews: an active partnership' in Ashdown, R., Carpenter, B. and Bovair, K. (Eds) *The Curriculum Challenge.* London: Falmer Press.

Mortimore, P., Sammons, P., Stoll, L., Lewis, D. and Ecob, R. (1988) *School Matters.* London: Open Books.

Reynolds, D. and Cuttance, P. (Eds) (1992) *School Effectiveness: research, policy and practice.* London: Cassell.

Russell, P. (1991) 'Access to the National Curriculum for Parents' in Ashdown, R. Carpenter, B. and Bovair, K. (Eds) *The Curriculum Challenge.* London: Falmer Press.

Wolfendale, S. (1988) *The Parental Contribution to Assessment.* Stratford-upon-Avon: NCSE.

Wolfendale, S. (1992) *Empowering Parents and Teachers.* London: Cassell.

Wolfendale, S. (1993) 'Involving parents in assessment' in Wolfendale, S. (Ed.) *Assessing Special Educational Needs.* London: Cassell.

Wolfendale, S. and Topping, K. J. (Eds) (1996) *Family Involvement in Literacy.* London: Cassell.

6 Parents as partners; some early impressions of the impact of the Code of Practice

Philippa Russell

> Paradoxically, the very advent and existence of the Code of Practice will test the parent–practitioner relationship to the full, in terms of attitudes, commitment and translation of the principles into action. The paradox lies in the fact that parental involvement in assessment and intervention has come so far as to be codified within a legislative framework and yet in being thus codified, the parent–professional relationship is now exposed. Pious hopes will be tested in reality, the scope and limitation of 'having regard to the provision of the Code' as well as the existence of new appeal arrangements will be explored by all concerned.
>
> (Wolfendale 1995, p.19)

Sheila Wolfendale's concept of a 'paradox' in terms of the Code of Practice's capacity to deliver the kind of positive partnership with parents envisaged within the drafting is an apt one. The Code of Practice does enshrine over a decade of developmental approaches to working with parents rather than seeing them as part of the 'problem' of their child's special needs. The Warnock Report (DES 1978) had heralded a new approach to parent involvement and the 1981 Act challenged previous preconceptions, not least in giving parents new rights to education. As one parent put it at the time:

> I felt I had really grown up. Suddenly I had the right to see all the advice on my child. I had the right to contribute my own advice and be sure it was circulated to all concerned. I hoped there would be no more secret decision-making behind closed doors.

But in practice the 1981 Act was more challenging than anyone (including parents) could have anticipated. Firstly, as both the Audit Commission (1992) and the House of Commons Education Committee on the implementation of the Act (1988) noted, the question of *support* for parents during assessment was never properly developed. Neither the role of the named person nor the contribution of the voluntary sector were formally acknowledged. Secondly resources were still allocated on an unclear basis and many families were preoccupied with *placement* rather than process and outcome measures. There was no independent appeal procedure and many LEAs noted that only a minority of parents really contributed to statutory assessment. Furthermore the concentration on the proverbial '2 per cent' failed to acknowledge that the vast majority, the 20 per cent, were left largely unrepresented and unsupported.

The 1993 Act was widely welcomed by parents. Many were concerned about resources in a down-turning economy, but the framework of the Code provided at last a principled approach to special educational needs. The advent of the SEN Tribunal signalled (at least in theory) more open decision making. The school-based stages of assessment and the long-awaited Individual Education Plan offered a more systematic approach to transition and review. The DFEE introduced Parent Partnership Schemes and, at last, the role of the Named Person became a reality. The introduction of school SEN policies was seen as a major advance in putting special educational needs on *every* school's agenda.

Two years on, has the Code of Practice made a difference? Statutory assessment is generally felt by parents to be more timely and focused. Many parents (as noted below) have welcomed the IEP and the SENCO, with his or her 'case-manager' role in schools. But expectations have also risen. Parents *expect* all their children to achieve. Schools have sometimes felt beleaguered with the constant pace of change. Also, Parent Partnership Schemes (discussed in several chapters) have proved more challenging than had originally been expected.

A key component within the Code of Practice was the expectation that schools and LEAs would acknowledge that effective special educational provision would not only necessitate partnerships with parents. It would expect new partnerships with health and social services. The SSI (Social Services Inspectorate) report on the first national inspection of services for disabled children (1994) highlighted the parallel challenge for social services departments, endeavouring to implement the Children Act 1989. SSI (1994) saw *educational* assessment as often the cornerstone of other assessment arrangements and speculated that integrated assessments around educational statutory assessments might be possible for the purposes of defining need for social or health services. Equally importantly, the report noted that families differ greatly, not only in their resources and their wishes and feelings about their children's development, but also in their past experience of professionals and the extent to which they can become 'partners' without support. Within the context of the 1993 Education Act and Code of Practice, the role of the Named Person was seen as an important enabling and advocacy role that should make a difference. The 1981 Act had reminded everyone that assessment is challenging, often time-consuming and frequently complex for parents without some form of personalised support.

Parent Partnership Schemes in action

Parent Partnership Schemes were a response to growing concerns within the consultation on the Code of Practice that the Code might 'founder' without a special befriending and representation role to support parents on their 'great adventures' within their children's assessment arrangements. The role of the Named Person had never been implemented in England (though was well bedded down in Scotland) and there was widespread recognition that the world had moved on since Warnock and the 1981 Act. Assessments now necessitated much more comprehensive assessment and review. The National Curriculum provided measurable achievements in education for all children. Additionally, wider concerns about legal indemnity in an increasingly litigious society and child protection issues made everybody very cautious about any new advocacy role. The voluntary sector, most articulate in their arguments for the implementation of the role of the Named Person (Russell 1996), thought again when asked to provide and to train large numbers of Named Persons without in most cases any additional resources. In effect parent partnership was, as one parent commented:

> Back on the drawing board ... with all the wisdom of hindsight I can see that the role of the named person was immensely more complex than we had originally envisaged back in the late 1980s. When we brainstormed [in a northern voluntary organisation] about the role of the named person, we came up with a job description which reqquired the patience and wisdom of the Angel Gabriel, the 'magic tricks' and the ability to drop in anywhere of Batman and the status of any powerful person who feels competent to 'take on the world.' But we were also aware that for some parents, power was not an important part of the equation. They literally wanted the comfortable 'person next door', to be a friend, to be there and just to help them enjoy their child. So, in thinking of training, we knew we needed versatility, empathy, communication and commitment. It took us a year to get our training scheme going, but it is all the better for the foundations we laid. We feel it has been an important process for everyone, including the LEA.
>
> (Personal communication 1996)

As Parent Partnership Schemes come to the end of their GEST funding, some important messages emerge. Firstly, implementation of the Code of Practice lays heavy time and resource commitments on everybody working with parents. Secondly, many parents find 'partnership' onerous. Thirdly, the role of the Named Person in the late 1990s requires training, support and a clear skill base which empowers but does not dominate; which is accessible and enabling and which sees the eventual autonomy of the *parent* (i.e. facilitating self-help) as a key objective. But, fourthly, there is also ample evidence coming back from the schemes that partnership often starts too late. OFSTED (1996a) noted the lack of information about Parent Partnership Schemes in schools. The school SEN policy has been a positive vehicle for change in some schools (particularly when parents have been able to inform and train their fellow governors). A sufficiency of Named Persons presupposes the resources to recruit, train and deploy them. Partnerships with the voluntary sector (particularly for children with low incidence disabilities) has not always been easy and many voluntary organisations are finding their traditional roles already over-burdened by increased demands and decreases in real resources. But the concept of partnership is there. The debate has moved on from statutory assessment to the school-based stages of assessment; annual reviews and the ongoing day-to-day life of schools where parents often have the most potential for making a difference.

The shift in balance of parent partnership is perhaps best illustrated by thinking about the function and effectiveness of the IEP and the all-important role of the SENCO in ensuring that parental involvement is indeed in the spirit of the Code and that early intervention is preferable to confrontation when things have gone badly wrong.

The Individual Education Plan

During the passage of the 1981 Education Act through parliament, there were powerful parental lobbies for the introduction of the Individual Education Plan, which was a key characteristic of planning for special educational needs in the USA. Many parents recognised that while the framework for statutory assessment had changed, assessment itself was unlikely to improve in terms of process and outcomes without specific individual planning. The IEP was rejected but was formally introduced within the Code of Practice. In practice, the involvement of parents (and their children) in the development, implementation and review of the IEP has been very variable. The Code of Practice envisaged parents being an integral part of the IEP process, with the plan specifying their own special contribution at home to help their child. The emphasis on target setting as part of the planning process was widely welcomed by parents and section 2.112 of the Code states that:

> The child's parents should always be informed of the action the school proposes to take ... The coordinator should agree with the child's teacher and any external specialists involved the arrangements for monitoring the child's progress against the targets established in the plan and should inform the child's parents about any special arrangements that will apply to their child and for how long.

The Code of Practice was explicit about the content of the IEP (section 2.119) noting that the plan should:

> develop, monitor, review and record, in consultation with parents and involving the child wherever possible ... such plans should include written information on individual programmes of work; performance targets; review dates, findings and decisions and parental involvement in and support for the plan.

The commitment to identifying children's strengths as well as weaknesses and to seeing parents as genuine partners in their children's education was warmly received. But as a Named Person (personal communication) commented:

> The IEP has raised expectations ... parents and teachers can feel pressured and anxious. There may be a temptation to underplay a child's strengths because, like the statement, the IEP may be seen as a means of accessing resources. Also joint planning is a major commitment. It takes time and energy and, speaking as

> a Named Person, I feel that to be really effective I would probably have the most impact if I could work with parents at stages two and three of assessment rather than at the 'hard end' of statutory assessment when in effect everything has gone wrong.

A parent, also concerned at the workload on all concerned, noted at a parent workshop:

> The Code of Practice was absolutely right about individual planning. But there can be a terrible pressure on everyone to record information and set targets for what the school can achieve with minimum effort. As a parent and a governor, I feel very guilty about expressing a wish for more than the school can easily deliver. I see all the paper work and one thing I am sure of – we need to decide what the minimum information should be within the IEP. We paid for our SENCO to go on a course, but she didn't find it much use. She feels that she is still photocopying lots of undigested paper because she isn't sure – and she hasn't the time – to produce a system. I know some of our parents have great difficulty in reading; really there's a lot of work to be done still about individual planning.

The concerns set out above reflect similar messages from the OFSTED report on the implementation of the Code of Practice (1996a). In section 106 OFSTED noted that: 'only in some schools are the IEP targets shared with parents and their views occasionally sought before the IEP is finalised'.

However, the same report noted encouragingly that a significant number of IEPs were now 'starting with a section encouraging staff to state the *positive* sides of a child's development (a frequent aspiration of parents who felt that assessment was frequently deficit laden) and that the involvement of *pupils* had led to some IEPs becoming 'often simpler and more manageable'.

The involvement of pupils within their own assessment and review arrangements was a major innovation within the Code of Practice, paralleling similar developments in involvement of children within social care and health planning. Implementation of the Children Act 1989 has indicated the real tensions which can arise when both children and parents are involved in significant decision-making, particularly with reference to disagreements about the best way forward. No research has as yet explored the implications for parents of a more pro-active involvement of children in assessment, but work around transition planning has indicated that many families are aware of the need to acknowledge that there may be disagreements and different targets at significant life stages. One parent (at a workshop on transition planning) noted that:

> The Carers (Recognition and Services) Act recognises that carers and people with disabilities may sometimes have different needs. Sometimes too much may be expected of parents and carers. 'Partnership' can mean ever-lasting programmes for the parents. Sometimes the children don't always want their parents badgering them to do this activity and that task! I would like two named persons around important times like transition planning. Some IEPs are really important because they feed into formal reviews. But really this can't happen unless the SENCO can act as a sort of care manager.

The role of the SENCO

The image of the SENCO as a 'care manager' is an apt one. Of all the new roles created or enhanced by the Code of Practice, the SENCO has had both the most possibilities and also the most pressure. The University of Warwick, in a report on a national survey of perceptions of SENCOs, carried out on behalf of the NUT, emphasises the challenges of implementing the role effectively, commenting that:

> The gulf between perceived expectations of the SENCO role in the light of the Code of Practice and the resources available to fill those expectations is likely to lead to increasing dissatisfaction from teachers, education managers, parents and school governors.
>
> (Lewis et al. 1996)

In the NUT report, a primary cause for concern was the limited 'non-contact time' for SENCOs and the need to look at systems within which a SENCO could flourish (i.e. standardising formats for IEPs and creating sustainable mechanisms for working across departments within schools). Teachers interviewed emphasised the challenge of what many felt to be 'bureaucratic dimensions' of making the Code of Practice work without additional resources. One SENCO commented that while she wished to write IEPs which were 'insightful, helpful and will result in change', she actually felt that:

> When there are a lot of children at Stages Two and Three, as in our case, fulfilling the requirements of IEP with parents, other parties and reviewing them every eight to ten weeks takes up a lot of lunchtimes!

A parent at a Council for Disabled Children workshop had a similar view, but felt that:

> Everything is very easily blamed on the Code of Practice. But really good schools had IEPs already, though they weren't necessarily called by that name. What the Code did was to provide a universal framework which has highlighted the gaps, as well as emphasising the positive. Teachers and SENCOs do need time to make the system work. But isn't that where School SEN Policies should work? I don't believe that sufficient governors really understand the importance of both non-teaching time and the calibre of person appointed to be the SENCO. I know a school where the main qualification was a licence to drive the school minibus!

The impact of the SEN Tribunal

Clearly the SENCO role will need to develop, if parents are to be meaningfully involved in assessment and planning at the earlier stages of the Code of Practice. John Wright of IPSEA, in evidence to the House of Commons Education Committee (1996) has noted the significant number of parents who choose their child's SENCO or class teacher as an expert witness for a hearing by the SEN Tribunal. Indeed a number of Parent Partnership Schemes have found parents not concerned by 'independent' named persons, but very anxious to have a familiar person at their child's school (often the SENCO) to perform the role on their behalf. Warnock had originally envisaged the child's teacher as a potential Named Person. But the world has moved on since 1978 and Wright identified the new phenomenon of the 'expert witness' who is fully prepared to speak for parents, but who may incur the wrath of the employing school or LEA in so doing. Wright (House of Commons 1996) identified a number of cases of intimidation of witnesses, with some teachers and SENCOs being forbidden to appear at tribunals, notwithstanding the power of the SEN Tribunal to subpoena them. But parents stressed the importance of having witnesses whom they trusted and who knew their children. One such witness (personal communication) commented that:

> I felt I had a duty to support ... at the Tribunal. After all, as one of her teachers and the SENCO for the school, I knew as much about her history as anyone else. Also I felt we had all worked very hard with the IEP, with target setting and review, and frankly we had really 'earned' a statutory assessment. But I did recognise there was a potential conflict of interest. I have a friend working in child protection and she told me to ask to be subpoenaed. She felt this was the only safe way and it saved red faces all round. But it was uncomfortable. I had some very awkward questions about the LEA.

The role of 'expert witness' may not have existed within the original concept of the Named Person's role, but parental expectations and the reality of the SEN Tribunal have highlighted the importance of:

- ensuring that parents are actively involved in very early assessment and planning so that they feel fully informed and confident about the level of intervention provided by the school – evidence from a study of parents going through 'due process' in the USA found that a high proportion ended up in formal legal procedures primarily because they felt uninformed about the basis for decision-making about their child.
- acknowledging that parents will need different *levels* of support (ranging from befriending and information through to advocacy and representation), all of which will require different skills. Some Parent Partnership Schemes are developing, or have established, conciliation services, acknowledging that significant numbers of referrals to the SEN Tribunal are withdrawn before a hearing and that *negotiation* should therefore be regarded as an integral part of the process of developing partnership with parents.

Has the SEN Tribunal made a difference? The 1981 Act introduced the concept of *rights* and *entitlement* into assessment. But without a formal and enforceable appeals process, parents commonly felt disenfranchised and disempowered. The 1993 Act provided the Tribunal (which has been generally welcomed and felt to be both fair and accessible). But good decisions do not necessarily achieve what parents feel to be 'justice'. Early evaluation of the work of the Tribunal has clearly demonstrated its very limited powers to enforce decisions. The increasing delegation of resources and autonomy to individual schools has left both the Tribunal and LEAs with minimal powers to enforce delivery of a decision. As one named person commented (personal communication):

> Parents can be desperately disappointed when they realise that getting the *place* they wanted, does not necessarily guarantee that the *support* will be delivered as they would have expected. In theory schools are now the embodiment of 'parent power'. But the 'parent power' is not always wholly committed to special needs. We still need to do a lot of work to make all schools really inclusive and to see the *investment* potential of special needs. I would like to see Parent Partnership Schemes and voluntary organisations working much more in schools – really like a sort of 'health education'! If we can't do this, we will end up being totally preoccupied with statements and with provision being driven by the most articulate parents. I believe in parents' rights, but I am really worried about a shift to a 'who is your lawyer' culture.

Creating and sustaining working partnerships with parents

The Named Person quoted above clearly states her concern to involve Parent Partnership Schemes earlier is shared by many of the schemes. But involvement is not resource neutral; it also presupposes awareness by schools of the importance of creating and sustaining working partnerships with parents. OFSTED (1996a) notes that:

> The idea of 'parents as partners' as used in the Code is sometimes mentioned in school documentation, often as an intention, but this is only at an early state in development in most schools ... a more proactive role in liaising with parents is severely restricted by lack of teachers' time. (p.26)

The same report goes on to observe that: 'Where the LEA has established parent partnership schemes, very little is known about them. Schools often do not even know of their existence. Few schools inform parents of the existence of these schemes and how to contact them' (p.27).

Even more worryingly, many of the parents in the schools covered by the survey did not have a Named Person even if the child had a statement. OFSTED also noted the real practical problem of part-time teaching staff, contracted by the hour, and the difficulty of managing a working partnership with parents in these circumstances – particularly if parent involvement meant what one teacher in the NUT survey described as 'the night-shift' or twilight-hour meetings.

However, problems in the quality of partnership as envisaged by the Code of Practice cannot always be simply allocated to schools. OPCS (1989), looking at disabled children in the UK, noted that no more than 35 per cent of parents belonged to a voluntary organisation. Many families had no idea that any relevant voluntary organisation or support group existed.

Ever since the implementation of the 1981 Act, LEAs, voluntary organisations and schools have acknowledged the real difficulties in supporting some parents in being involved in assessment and planning for their children. As the Fish Committee noted (ILEA 1985), some parents have had very poor experiences themselves of the education system. They have no personal model of 'partnership' to build upon. Other parents may have insufficient time to be involved or may misunderstand the contribution expected of them. OFSTED (1996a) also notes that 'When schools have produced courses or special evenings for parental in-service training on the Code, staff have usually been disappointed by poor levels of attendance' (p.26).

OFSTED also noted that when schools had invited parents to staff INSET on the Code, parents often found this well intentioned but 'daunting'. The messages are clear. Many parents need to acquire confidence in developing new roles in schools and with their children's individual teachers. Parent Partnership Schemes, while originally created to primarily support statutory assessments and reviews, have a continuing and potentially important role with schools. But their own resource limitations mean that they too will need to find new ways of supporting *groups* of parents rather than individual parents on a highly selective basis.

The school SEN policy

The impact of school SEN policies on individual school approaches to parent involvement has yet to be fully evaluated. But informal evidence from Parent Partnership Schemes and the member organisations of the Council for Disabled Children suggests that many parents with children with special needs *are* using the process of developing and reviewing a policy as an opportunity to address the creation of more positive roles for parents.

Circular 6/94, on the organisation of special educational provision, states that schools SEN policies should state:

- information on parents' involvement in assessment and decision-making, emphasising the importance the school places on their contribution;
- any local or national voluntary organisations which provide support or advice for parents;
- arrangements for recording and acting upon parental concerns;
- procedures for involving parents when a concern is first registered by the school;
- arrangements for incorporating parents' views in assessment and subsequent reviews.

Schools are also reminded in both circular and Code of Practice that they should consider *access* for parents as an important issue, making sure that they provide information for parents whose first language is not English or who may have communication and literacy problems. Schools are also reminded of the value of a parents' room or other arrangements to make parents feel comfortable about coming into school. The issue of access will become more challenging when the Disability Discrimination Act 1995 is implemented and schools will be required to state clearly what access arrangements they make for disabled people (children and adults – hence including parents) and any anti-discriminatory measures which they propose to implement.

Some schools have used the requirement to develop a policy to involve actively the whole school community (teachers, governors and parents) in developing a pro-active approach to meeting special educational needs. Where the parent governor is interested (or indeed the parent of a child with a disability or special need), there have been some exciting developmental approaches – acknowledging that achieving an effective school policy will be 'developmental and incremental and that the *process* is as important as the final paper product. Governor training is clearly a critical issue, and as one governor commented (CDC seminar):

> It was not until I started training that I realised how all pervasive special educational needs are. I admit I had seen special needs as just one more task for governors. I had not seen the importance for schools of adopting a confident and inclusive approach towards all our pupils. Most importantly I realised that most children with special needs are not specially placed from outside our schools. They are there already! I also realised some of the stresses that parents experience, their fear of rejection and the need to convey clear messages about our confidence and competence to work in this area and our commitment to all our children.

Special Educational Needs in context

The comment on *all our children* is particularly salutary when reflecting that special educational needs may result from the child's interaction with his or her wider family and community environment. As OFSTED noted in *Access and Achievement in Urban Education:*

> Beyond the school gate are underlying social issues such as poverty, unemployment, poor housing, inadequate health care and the break-up of families. Education by itself can only do so much to enable individuals to reach beyond the limiting contours of their personal and social circumstances and succeed.
>
> (1994, p.35)

In effect, creating a more sensitive approach to real consumer involvement in special educational needs will be ineffective without attention being paid to the whole lives of families and the frequently associated social disadvantages which can create major barriers to active partnerships.

Baldwin and Carlisle (1994), reviewing the research literature on the lives of disabled children and their families, noted that many families are not *really* coping. In practice they experience and meet their problems to the best of their abilities and often face secondary difficulties as a result. It is often the *accumulation* of a wide range of problems which disturbs relationships; inhibits parental involvement in educational and other activities and which can disturb the relationships between parents and professionals. As Baldwin and Carlisle comment, 'The real problem may be seen as family pathology, but actually the *real* challenge is how to provide practical assistance and support in ways which are compatible with family lifestyles and commitment' (1994, p.15).

They go on to note that the need for information, advice and counselling is ongoing and needs to take account of families' current circumstances and past histories. As one family noted at a Council for Disabled Children workshop:

> Some of us families collect professionals like other people collect stamps. But knowing 17 different professionals isn't partnership. It's a survival exercise with often conflicting advice, everyone with expectations and a bag of homework at the end of the day that makes you feel you should be the real professionals! Family life is partnership too.

Perhaps the last word should rest with the views of a group of north of England parents about their children with disabilities and special needs:

- Please accept and value our children (and ourselves as families) as we are.
- Please celebrate difference!
- Please try and accept our children as children first. Don't attach labels to them unless you mean to *do* something
- Please recognise your power over our lives. We live with the consequences of your opinions and decisions
- Please understand the stress many families live under. The cancelled appointment, the waiting list no-one gets to the top of, all the discussions about resources – it's *our* lives you are talking about!
- Don't push fashionable fads and treatments on to us unless you are going to be around to see them through! And don't forget families have many members, many responsibilities. Sometimes we can't please everyone.
- Do recognise that sometimes we are right! Please believe us and listen to what know we and our child need.
- Sometimes we are sad, tired and depressed. Please value us as caring and committed families and try to go on working with us.

The Code of Practice has made a difference in terms of parental participation in the assessment and review of their children's special educational needs. Where the pressures have occurred, they have not reflected the inadequacies of the Code, but rather the Code's clarification of the conditions (and the resource implications) for effective parental participation. In many respects, the Code has also challenged what we mean by parent partnership. A report on the lives of families with severely disabled children (Beresford 1995) clearly demonstrated that while parents wanted accurate information, informed decision-making, respect and inclusion, many also felt over-burdened by expectations about their roles as co-therapists and workers.

Phil Madden (1995), looking at a decade of parent partnership, comments that notwithstanding very positive commitments to working *with* parents across all three statutory services:

> Many professionals continue to suffer from 'parentitis' – a mixture of prejudice, ambivalence and ignorance of the strengths, concerns and insights of parents ... one wonders whether some of the protracted and bloody battles that take place between agencies and individual parents (which often have pyrrhic outcomes) could have been avoided if professionals had behaved from the start with more empathy.

A key objective in the Code of Practice was that of mutual understanding and negotiation, a recognition that process is as important as outcomes and that partnership with parents will always be challenging. OFSTED (1996b), looking at achievement for pupils with special educational needs in mainstream schools, saw 'working partnerships' as a characteristic of successful schools. Perhaps the key message of the Code of Practice is that we will continue learning about the real meaning of partnership – and that parents, as well as professionals, have responsibilities for clarity, sensitivity and commitment in helping education services to be more effective in meeting *their* needs in the best interests of children.

References

Audit Commission (1992) *Getting in on the Act.* London: HMSO.

Baldwin, S. and Carlisle, J. (1994) *Social Support for Disabled Children and their Families: a review of the literature.* Edinburgh: Social Work Services Inspectorate/ HMSO.

Beresford, B. (1995) *Expert Opinions: families with severely disabled children.* York: Joseph Rowntree Foundation/SPRU, University of York.

DES (1978) *Special Educational Needs,* Report of the Committee of Inquiry into Special Educational Needs, chair Baroness Warnock. London: HMS0.

DFEE (1994) *The Code of Practice on the Identification and Assessment of Special Educational Needs.* London: HMSO.

DFEE (1994) *Organisation of Special Educational Provision* Circular 6/94. London: HMSO.

Duckworth, D. and Philp, J. (1982) *Children with Disabilities and their Families: a review of the literature.* Windsor: NFER–Nelson.

House of Commons (1991) *Report of Committee of Inquiry into the Implementation of the 1981 Education Act.* London: House of Commons.

ILEA (1985) *Equal Opportunities for All?* Report of the Committee of Inquiry into Special Educational Provision in London, chair John Fish. London: Inner London Education Authority.

Lewis, A., Neil, S. and Campbell, R. (1996) *The Implementation of the Code of Practice in Primary and Secondary Schools: a national survey of perceptions of special educational needs co-ordinators.* Warwick: NUT/University of Warwick.

Madden, P. (1995) 'Parents as Partners: a new perspective' *British Journal of Learning Disabilities,* 23, pp.23–7, British Institute of Learning Disabilities.

Office of Population and Census Surveys (1989) *Report 6, Disabled Children: services, transport and education.* London: HMSO.

OFSTED (1994) *Access and Achievement in Urban Education.* London: HMSO.

OFSTED (1996a) *The Implementation of the Code of Practice for Pupils with Special Educational Needs*. London: HMSO.

OFSTED (1996b) *Promoting High Achievement: evaluation of pupils with special educational needs in mainstream schools.* London: HMSO.

Russell, P. (1996) *The Role of the Named Person.* Council for Disabled Children, 8 Wakley St, London EC1V TQE.

Social Services Inspectorate (1994) *Report of the First National Inspection of Services for Children with Disabilities.* London: HMSO.

Wolfendale, S. (1995) 'Parental Involvement' in Stobbs, P. (Ed.) *Schools Special Educational Needs Policy Pack.* London: National Children's Bureau.

7 A review of Parent Partnership Schemes

Teresa Furze and Anna Conrad

Introduction and background

This chapter provides an overview of some of the developments taking place and future directions in Parent Partnership Schemes since provision of GEST funding. GEST stands for Grants for Education, Support and Training. It is used by the Department for Education and Employment to 'pump prime' 'training and development initiatives in LEAs. GEST funding for SEN Parent Partnership Schemes has been provided for three years, with April 1996 to April 1997 being the final year. Bids from LEAs were submitted to the DFEE of which 60 per cent of the funding came from GEST and 40 per cent from the LEA . Most LEAs in England applied for and received funding, the bids in this final year ranging from £300 for the City of London to £116,000 for Coventry. (Actual allocations have ranged from £300 to £97,000 for Nottinghamshire.) Over the three years the total allocated by the DFEE has been £11.3 million.

The context of schemes

There are some 21 titles for the GEST-funded post holders. For the purposes of this chapter they will all be referred to as Parent Partnership Officers (PPOs)and their schemes as Parent Partnership Schemes (although some have a narrower brief with their emphasis on development of a Named Person scheme).

The range of previous posts, experience and qualifications of PPOs was as wide as their salaries which ranged from below £15,000 to over £30,000. Twenty per cent of schemes had no administrative support. Schemes range from those with no PPO, to those with a PPO, project workers, helpline workers and administrative staff (full time or part time). Most PPOs were, and still are, based in education departments.

The yearly nature of the GEST bidding has meant that many PPOs are on yearly contracts, with some being secondments from other posts. This has not, however, prevented a handful of LEAs showing their commitment by making permanent appointments, notably Hertfordshire and Nottinghamshire who both advertised nationally. Some LEAs, for example Redbridge, have recently appointed – others do not intend to appoint.

Besides the budgets allocated to them, a number of factors may have affected the progress of schemes including; parents' centres in place; regular SEN forums involving parents, voluntary organisations and various agencies; as well as good LEA contacts with voluntary organisations. A strong commitment to community education and cultures which promote parent partnership work (for example, LEAs with policies in place on parental involvement) have also played their part. Other factors that have probably contributed are the detail and degree of consultation with interested parties, before making bids, which meant that LEAs were able to make an early, credible appointment.

Most PPOs are line managed by an officer or advisor from within their education department. In over half there was a steering/management group, but in many of these there was no clear remit and not all the interested parties are members. The effects of these groups has been debatable and sometimes dependent on personalities. Very few, for example Avon, Bury, Bradford, Lancashire, Warwickshire, East Sussex are managed by the voluntary or community sector. The latter has enabled the work to be developed with a fair amount of independence while still ensuring that the LEA is involved in developing the partnership. In the case of Bradford, Barnardo's contributed £20,000 to the funding of the scheme bringing additional benefits. (Some LEAs, such as Hampshire have given out small grants for specific purposes to voluntary organisations for example, to develop an independent helpline and for resources to be lent to parents.)

There is no doubt that the issue of independence was, and in some cases still is, of major concern to many parents and voluntary organisations in their local communities (equally the independence of voluntary organisations advocating their own special schools to parents is an issue to education departments). However, where a PPO has been resourced and well placed within the hierarchy of the Education Department they can put forward the parental perspective and effect change from within (particularly by facilitating a more co-ordinated and efficient approach i.e. getting different services/departments to work together). Many PPOs within Education Departments believe that they have been able to resolve difficulties because of their easy access to files, relevant information and education personnel. One PPO has reflected that being based outside the Education Department has possibly contributed to the difficulties of persuading the LEA to improve its communication with parents.

Differing degrees of independence have been developed. Ealing, for instance, has distanced itself from the day-to-day management of the scheme to being involved solely in personnel issues, such as annual leave. The appointment of the PPO and management of the scheme has been carried out by a steering group with independent professional support for the PPO bought in from the Senjit Parent Partnership Consortium. In other cases LEAs have separated the line management within the education department, for example, in Knowsley the PPO is line managed by the senior assistant director (strategic support) not by the assistant director (student services) who is the Named Officer's line manager.

The late inclusion of the Named Person role in the Code meant PPOs had been appointed for their knowledge and skills in the special needs area rather than particular experience of setting up and running volunteer schemes. Additionally they had no budgets for expenses etc. Consequently 'Named Persons' hijacked the debate on areas that needed addressing. To some extent this, unfortunately, continues to be the case.

Named Person schemes (see Code of Practice paragraph 4: 70 – 4: 73)

Many PPOs have looked to the voluntary sector and Scotland for models to develop their schemes: particularly, the Voluntary Centre UK, Elfrida Rathbone, Special Needs Advisory Project (SNAP) and Supportive Parents for Special Children (SPSC) (see Robina Mallett, Chapter 3).

Where Named Person schemes are being developed they have done so to differing degrees. This has probably been dependent on their resources, the local response of voluntary organisations, the commitment to the concept and practicalities of its implementation, and the attitude of LEAs. Many LEAs found lack of co-operation from the voluntary sector, who were not prepared to act as Named Persons concerned about the legal implications of providing wrongful advice, and adding further demands to their already stretched resources. This was not the case in all areas of the country, for example Islington consulted a wide range of voluntary organisations. A number agreed to make available officers and members to take on the Named Person role and were provided with some training from an independent consultant and packs of materials.

Other LEAs simply consulted the voluntary organisations and made up a list of those prepared to act as Named Persons and sometimes sent them packs. The majority have found it difficult to recruit Named Persons from the voluntary sector. The numbers of Named Persons that schemes have on their books range from less than a handful to around 100 with a few having more.

Those schemes that have successfully recruited have advertised widely with posters, articles, press releases, leaflets, word of mouth (and spoken to any relevant group or organisation that will listen!) as well as using volunteer bureaux. Newspaper adverts and articles, have in some cases increased response ten-fold. Some also ask colleagues in the Education Department, health and social services, to nominate parents they know who might be suitable and willing to become volunteers. Offering training and support has probably been critical in keeping the interest of volunteers. Accreditation of Named Person schemes is likely to increase recruitment as well as build in quality assurance.

Many LEAs are explaining the role of the Named Person at Code of Practice Stage Four, with most identifying someone by Stage Five. The actual demand for Named Persons is difficult to generalise. In some authorities 5 per cent of parents are providing their own Named Persons, in others considerably more. Where the parents themselves have not named someone, most LEAs are identifying a person for advice and information who is frequently the PPO or the LEA Named Officer, sometimes the educational psychologist, specialist teacher, a member of the Education Welfare Service (EWS), or the headteacher of the child's school. The potential for conflict of interest is of particular concern in the case of the headteacher. A number of LEAs are not naming anyone if this is the parent's wish. Evaluations have shown that some parents regard it as an insult to their intelligence to have a Named Person.

Some issues

The range of people becoming Named Persons has been dependent on their LEA's policies. Some LEAs are agreeable to employees becoming Named Persons. Generally in these cases they are stipulating the Named Person should not be the case worker for that child or involved in that child's school. Most Named Persons come from the group of parents/carers, retired LEA personnel (from directors downwards), voluntary organisation workers, social services department, Portage homeworkers, preschool playgroup association workers, schools governors, teachers from travelling services, retired teachers and ethnic minority groups. Most Named Persons are women.

The need for Named Persons to reflect the cultural and language diversity found in an LEA has proved to be a challenge, met in Tower Hamlets by employing bilingual staff to take on the role of Named Person.

Schemes range greatly in how many volunteers go on to be Named Persons from 0 to 100 per cent, both between and within schemes. However, in many cases the volunteers felt they would use the knowledge and skills gained, which is likely to feed into the informal network of support for parents. Some evaluations of Named Persons schemes (Devon, Essex) suggest that peer support is fairly critical in both recruiting and retaining Named Persons in addition to any support provided by the PPO. It is early days to be clear on the drop-out rate, but Enfield has found it to be roughly 25 per cent.

Surprisingly insurance has been a significant issue despite volunteers being used widely in LEAs whether they are governors or parents working in schools. Well-developed schemes have ensured that their volunteers have full information about their insurance cover, as well as offering them guidance in terms of working in ways to reduce the risk of any claims arising.

Well-developed schemes have person specifications, job descriptions, application forms and contracts. Such schemes clarify what is expected of Named Persons as well as what they can expect in support and training. In addition they have equal opportunity policies, codes of conduct and procedures for managing the change of a Named Person, as well as complaints procedures and detailed record sheets to be completed by Named Persons, and forms for claiming expenses (Devon provides B/T chargecards) (see Chapter 8). Schemes now have a range of literature helping parents identify their own Named Person.

Training and support for Named Persons

A number of schemes are now into a cycle of publicity, training and selection. The good schemes recognise their three-fold responsibility:

1 to the users (parents) to make sure that their existing situation is not made any worse;

2 to the volunteers to prevent them getting out of their depth;

3 to the scheme itself to ensure that its credibility and its standards remain as high as possible.

Many schemes are clear about the kind of person they are looking for and would probably agree with the list in the Scottish Befriending Development Forum Resources Pack (see in References).

Good schemes make clear that not everybody may be suitable but there are other jobs that they could do to support the scheme. Schemes have varied in their use of police checks and some have ID cards (Bromley). Many schemes recognise that this issue cannot be isolated from the wider process of which it forms a part i.e. the process of recruitment, training, selection, placement, support and supervision which go a long way to ensure protection for all those who need it (parents, Named Persons and Parent Partnership Schemes).

The amount of training ranges widely from one or two sessions, a series of five, ten or more sessions over a period of weeks, a solid two or three days, or very extensive fourteen week training programmes – some with regular homework and portfolios of work. (Lancashire and Cumbria are developing accreditation through the local Open Colleges.)

To enable some degree of independence(and allow the PPO to concentrate on assessing volunteers) much of the training has been via independent organisations or by using their training materials. LEA personnel are being used simply to explain administrative procedures, SEN policy and provision in the area.

Content of training has ranged through understanding how a scheme works and the qualities involved in being a Named Person, through to understanding of the Code of Practice, statutory assessment and roles and responsibilities of professionals within it, as well as development of skills in working with parents, development of awareness of self. Child protection issues and training on specific tasks that may be needed for some parents as well as issues to do with working in the home have also often been included. Schemes have varied in whether they are developing training on tribunal support. Some prefer to use only a select few who are trained up to become representatives at tribunals. Others cover this area because the volunteers involved want to carry on supporting parents through to tribunal.

Matching tends to be the responsibility of the PPO using criteria such as availability, geographical location, safety of routes used, linguistic, cultural and sometimes political background, knowledge of the child's special needs, the particular skills of the Named Person, and their training, as well as a PPO's 'intuition'.

In some schemes where parents have already unburdened themselves to the PPO it has been very difficult to effect matches despite them appearing ideal as the parents do not wish to unburden themselves to someone else yet again. This has obvious implications for the way schemes are organised in their contact with parents, but also explains why many parents are loath to take on yet another person when they are already being bombarded with many professionals.

Support for Named Persons has varied through individual support and supervision by PPOs with access to: telephone support; regular support groups to encourage airing of problems, discuss changes, share ideas and inform the PPO of issues facing the volunteers and plan further training; buddying/mentor schemes; resource libraries; newsletters; social functions; and information packs. Supervision may be carried out through these groups and via individual telephone conversations and occasionally through joint visiting. For any scheme to have credibility, it needs to be in regular contact with its Named Persons and to build in systems for doing this. The written contract or agreement between the Named Person scheme and volunteers can be a basis for a review either at regular intervals or when circumstances change.

The future

Only a few schemes have been independently evaluated so far, for example East Sussex, but many are building in evaluation. Most LEA's subjective feedback suggests that parents are finding Named Persons useful. Formal feedback in Enfield found that all parents found the scheme useful.

However, OFSTED, in their 1996 report found that parents of pupils with Statements were usually unaware of any Named Person and often of the Named Officer within the LEA. Some of those with more recent Statements issued since the Code had been introduced could identify the Named LEA Officer but information about the Named Person had not been sent with the final statement.

Looking to the future it seems highly unlikely that schemes will be able to recruit, train, support and retain people in sufficient numbers to meet the new Statements, never mind for support in annual reviews, transition plans etc. In addition a number of parents would prefer to receive support from a parent support group rather than a Named Person or from their voluntary group with which they are already involved. A recent DFEE letter August 96 now allows for a more flexible approach. Greater clarity though is needed about the role and responsibilities of the Named Person (and a less confusing title!). Many more voluntary organisations or support groups would be willing to become Named Persons if the use of the term 'advice' was clarified. In addition, promotion of support from employers (as for school governors) would increase the availability of Named Persons during the day and their status.

Many refer to the system of identifying a Named Person at the end of the statutory assessment process as 'shutting the stable door after the horse has bolted'. Many schemes have recognised this and are endeavouring to provide and make available Named Persons from Stage Four. More need to consider the advisability of developing, befrienders /Named Persons at Stages One to Three as in Devon, and support groups for parents based in schools as in Knowsley, so that there is a continuum of support for parents.

The Named Officer (see Code of Practice paragraphs 3:101, 4:67, 4:73, 6:12)

One always needs to bear in mind that the number of Named Persons needed in practice will, to a great extent, depend on the quality of information, support and advice provided by the professionals and LEA education officers, particularly the Named Officer.

Many Parent Partnership Schemes have been disseminating examples of innovative practice to facilitate the process of LEAs working out what would best meet the needs of their parents within their current system and resources. Some of the very simple techniques that have been advocated for years, for example, to telephone parents at the beginning of the statutory assessment to introduce themselves, and again at the critical stages to check rather than wait for an anxious parent to telephone them are now becoming regular good practice.

The Named Officer and LEA officers need no longer be the 'faceless bureaucrats' of the past. For example, in Redbridge all parents are invited to visit the education office to meet with their assessment officer who explains the process, answers any concerns that the family may have, and gives information on the Named Person and advice on local voluntary groups. Parents are again invited to discuss the contents of their statement with the officer. In Westminster Named Officers make home visits when needed. Hertfordshire along with its established Parents Advisory Group and PPO have delivered and evaluated seminars for parents at the beginning of the statutory assessment procedures. A number of LEAs pre-1993 Education Act had already developed approaches where for example, parents are invited to panel meetings, or where parents draft their child's Statement together with their Named Officer.

Lack of clarity with the roles of Named Persons and Named Officers abound. The need for a more pro-active rather than re-active role is recognised. At a Senjit Parent Partnership Consortium Conference in December

1995 (SENJIT 1995), most participants (LEA officers, parents, voluntary organisations, PPOs) felt that there should be clear LEA policies and procedures to make the role more effective. Most also felt that Named Officers needed training in working with parents, negotiation skills, awareness of disability, knowledge of relevant legislation, local schools and provision among others. Free-standing training packs in similar areas, were also felt to be helpful. The potential for joint training with parents, other Named Officers and Named Persons was recognised. Support and resources that were felt to be needed included local support groups, resource libraries, helplines.

In a few Parent Partnerships Schemes, PPOs are taking a lead role in helping Named Officers analyse their own development and training needs, and organising training and support to match these (Essex). In the Senjit Parent Partnership Consortium a support group for Named Officers has been developed which is to be offered to all the LEAs within the main Senjit Consortium.

Many of the needs for training, support and resources overlap with those of the Named Person which has clear implications for the developing role of PPOs, and may also provide an additional source of funding.

Information for parents

Many Parent Partnership Schemes have spent a large proportion of their time developing packs of information for parents and Named Persons as well as supporting LEAs and redrafting their letters to parents. Most have done so with varying levels of parental input. Compared to pre-1993 Act there is now a wealth of literature ranging through parent's rights and responsibilities, parental representation and contributions, explanations of the various aspects of the Code of Practice and the 1993 Act and its local implementations such as the stages of assessments, annual reviews and transition plans. Areas include tribunals and complaints procedures, guides to the various disabilities, the LEAs SEN policies and funding systems for SEN, the role of the Named Person, the role of the Named Officer and Parent Partnership Scheme brochures. The usual glossaries, useful books and addresses, local voluntary and national organisation lists and lists of schools are included.

Some of the literature is extremely practical and helpful to parents, such as ways to keep organised, keep track of paperwork and appointments, questions to ask the professionals involved in the assessment, questions to ask and things to do when visiting schools, ways to identify a Named Person, detailed guidance on escorts and transport. Much of the above was available some ten years or so ago. The advent of PPOs has facilitated their use and dissemination and enabled them to be built upon. An additional area needs to be included of helping parents elicit their own child's views and ways to deal with conflict, building on approaches such as those in Waltham Forest.

Schemes have also developed various feedback mechanisms to improve their literature. In Hampshire materials are being sold with discs so they can be easily adapted to local needs without reinventing the wheel. Oxfordshire has recently put all its information for parents on the Internet.

Ways round the great cost of translating all booklets developed are being tackled in some schemes by developing a bank of audio tapes of the literature. This also overcomes the difficulty of a parent speaking a language but not being literate in it.

In addition many PPOs have developed resource banks of literature and materials for themselves, parents and Named Persons. The RNIB and Elfrida Rathbone Manchester and ACE booklets are particularly useful. Databases of local and national voluntary organisations have been a priority for many schemes with some using Dissbase, a computer programme produced by the Disability Information Service which is updated yearly for a fee. Some are reaching agreement with library and information services to develop an accessible system for all. Database development is very expensive, but developing and updating the cost of these could be shared between neighbouring authorities where local voluntary groups often overlap.

Despite the great activity in this area, however, there are still examples of literature where the readability is too high, the print too small, although the actual content covered may be good. The actual process that some LEAs have gone through in drafting materials needs reviewing particularly the range of educational background of parents consulted, the writer's skills in plain English and use of computer programmes on readability. There are some good ideas about: Calderdale have literacy advisory panels; Kensington and Chelsea have lists of a range of parents from differing backgrounds who are willing to give feedback; Leeds Parent Partnership Scheme gathered over 100 people (all at the same time) from parent, voluntary organisations, and professionals to go through and draft literature together in groups facilitating wider ownership and commitment to the development of information for parents.

Roughly a third of schemes have developed helplines, some with minicom. Some are staffed by volunteers who have generally been offered training and support. Some (e.g. Hampshire) have provided or are considering providing help to voluntary organisations to enable them to develop sustainable and independent helplines for parents of children with SEN. Many LEAs include cover for the helpline as in all their cover for all volunteers and LEA personnel. Advice lines support parents and also provide representative picture of parental concerns. Where detailed monitoring of the calls occurs (e.g. in Avon) this information can be incorporated into service delivery.

Provision of information to parents has included development of a number of videos covering various stages of the Code, for example Coventry '1 in 5' for children on Stages One to Three: the Leeds video *Breaking down the Barriers* concentrating on the statutory assessment and the Knowsley video on describing provision within Knowsley. The Coventry and Leeds videos are available with subtitles and in British Sign Language (BSL) and a number of languages.

Monitoring is critical to ensuring the effectiveness of a distribution network. There is a need for the central research and information dissemination to help prevent reinventing the wheel. Hertfordshire county library service is one of the first to join the Internet. Better use of IT particularly CD-ROM in devising, developing, disseminating, and increasing accessibility of leaflets/videos is needed. The development of clear guidelines for all LEAs and useful resources, use of more sophisticated piloting such as observation of reader behaviour to infer changes are needed. Training workshops run along the lines of the Plain English campaign with those who are producing or wish to produce information for parents should be standard.

Work with individual parents

A great deal of individual work has been carried out by PPOs mainly in the role of Named Person via helplines, meetings with parents, discussing their contribution, visiting schools with them, putting the families in contact with voluntary organisations, typing up drafts, assisting with form filling, advising on information to include and generally giving support and guidance. Often PPOs attend meetings and write letters as well as provide SEN tribunal support. Besides helplines some PPOs are offering individual support for parents by drop-in clinics and mobile clinics in schools.

One would hope that all PPOs would have some regular contact with parents on an individual basis when they are going through the assessment procedures. However, the proportion of time allocated to this in many schemes, has clearly limited development in the other areas of work.

Conciliation and mediation

In some LEAs parents have the benefit of a second opinion from the EPS. LEAs such as Southwark and Essex have such schemes. In Hertfordshire private EP advice is bought in. Some parents are buying in second opinions privately, some cannot afford this. Most would agree that the better advice often comes from those who know the child from their work within the child's school. PPOs are in an ideal position to bring this area to the attention of LEA officers in order to promote a system for second opinions within or across LEAs.

The areas of mediation and conciliation in Hertfordshire and Somerset have been brought more and more to the attention of schemes and their LEAs. Parents are more likely to have confidence when those providing such a service are not involved in the provision of the service for example PPO or different departments of the LEA.

Schools

The recent OFSTED report (1996) highlighted that little is known about Parent Partnership Schemes. Schools often did not know of their existence. Few schools informed parents of their existence and how to contact them.

This report also noted that staff and governors found one of the most difficult aspects was reporting to parents the success of the SEN policy in their schools. The requirement that parents should be informed when their child is included in the SEN register was not fully understood by schools. Neither was the importance of collecting clear evidence when they wished to request help at Stages Three and Four for their pupils – through copies of letters and the logging of conversations with parents at Stages One and Two. (This was especially so in secondary schools.) It found that developing the idea of parents as partners as set out in the Code of Practice was frequently mentioned in school documentation, but in reality was an intention requiring far more development; particularly involving parents in formulating and reviewing Individual Education Plans. It was also unusual to find that the views of the parents had been canvassed in formulating the SEN policy unless this was part of traditional policy development in schools.

There is a clear need to shift work in the direction of prevention which in the long run will make more effective use of resources. This may prove a useful avenue for future funding. PPOs could have a clear role in developing pro-active work within school for example, in developing – complaints procedures, ways to communicate effectively and constructively with parents both in writing and verbally, effective ways for parent governors to represent parents' views, and teachers' home–school liaison. PPOs could contribute to training on these areas and in the development of interest and support groups as well as helping schools develop resources to support parents and use local voluntary organisation support more effectively. Some projects such as Knowsley are working with selected schools to pilot programmes to encourage school-based SEN parent groups. For example, in Knowsley two mainstream and two special schools have offered training to groups of parents with children with SEN in order to enable them to better support those parents whose children have been newly identified as having SEN. PPOs could support development of home–school policies in full consultation with parents, and plans for making SEN policies and other policies readily available to parents, involving them in its development and consulting them over IEPs.

Schools are more likely to be welcoming of approaches where they see this fulfilling their needs to improving the school system for working with *all* parents.

Policy

An important area that Parent Partnership Schemes need to focus their attention on in this final year, if parents are really to be brought into the partnership in making decisions about their child, is to make LEAs agree that they are entitled to ask questions about the overall resource framework and way decisions are made about their child. PPOs can also contribute the overall parental perspective to help to develop a system that is clear, accountable and fair to parents.

ACE (1996) has drawn attention to the fact that many LEAs had not considered the issue of transport and had ad-hoc policies which were not communicated to parents in advance. Parental involvement in annual reviews often involved travelling for parents and perhaps overnight stays. Their survey revealed that many LEAs were not aware of the full range of issues that were important to parents and that in some authorities either policy did not exist or no one had anticipated the issues. This is clearly an area where Parent Partnership Schemes should have some input for example in advocating simple good practice (for example parents and LEA representative where possible travelling together). Perhaps more importantly PPOs need to support LEAs in establishing clear policies at LEA level for parent partnership work.

Other areas of Parent Partnership Schemes activities

Many schemes have canvassed parents' views on Stages Four and Five procedures before and after the 1993 Education Act. Together LEAs and schemes have developed ongoing feedback systems, some where parental views are sampled, some where every parent is asked for their comments at the end of the statutory assessment. Only a few have sought out the parental perspective of the Stages Zero to Three (Islington). Where surveys have included requests for parental support from parents responses have been positive, for example, in Haringey 50 per cent of parents who replied volunteered to be Named Persons.

Other significant activities have included one-off training for teachers, governors, LEA officers, child development centres, SENCO, educational psychologists, development of self-managing support groups and information days for parents.

Where schemes have held events for parents, asked parents about their needs, and how to meet these, for example via crèches, timing of meetings, availability of interpreters, induction loops, accessibility of meeting venues, a friend with them to help and so on, this has created a far greater and wider representation of parents. Where parents have also helped with setting the agenda, planning and carrying out the day this has been successful. Some schemes, for example, SPSC Avon have well-developed forums for sharing of good practice which are open to parents, governors, LEA officers and professionals which are very popular. Local forums for sharing good practice need to become a key feature of all schemes, so that parents and LEAs can see each other in a different light and open up communication.

It is important for PPOs to consider developing mechanisms within their LEAs to keep parent partnership on the agenda formally once GEST is finished, for example, by facilitating a broadly based group, consisting of representatives from councillors, voluntary and parents groups, ethnic minority groups, health and social services, LEA and schools with its own remit so that it continues to develop. This would enable a culture to be continued and developed where parents are always consulted in the development of LEA plans that affect their children.

Monitoring and evaluation

Many schemes produce regular reports to line managers and steering committees, giving details of progress towards each of the objectives of their scheme where these have been clearly articulated (quantity of literature produced, numbers of Named Persons recruited, aspects of the schemes in place, insurance scheme/system clarified databases developed etc.). Being able to answer questions such as if the scheme is helpful, what parents want and need and is useful to the LEA is less evident. Some schemes have well-developed databases where they can show the numbers of telephone enquiries, response times, level and type of demand, referral routes, the age of children and their special needs, the action, advice and outcomes and incorporate ethnic monitoring. Some schemes are evaluating their training well with pre- and post-training questionnaires about the extent to which the training has met the needs, has been successfully delivered, and identified future needs.

Many schemes still are not monitoring whether there is an increased percentage of parental representations and contributions and whether these contributions are changing in their amount, detail and quality. Appeal rates and in some case length of time to reach agreement are being recorded in many LEAs. Evaluation of the distribution of newsletters to see if some schools are better at delivering information to parents has been carried out in one or two LEAs.

Besides evaluating what parents think of the scheme some have also included in evaluations what the other partners feel about the schemes, particularly voluntary organisations. Only a few schemes have set aside a portion of their budget for evaluation work, for example Tower Hamlets, Somerset, Newham. Others have managed to negotiate with local university departments, for example, Knowsley, or through Business in the Community, for example, East Sussex. The latter were able to carry out an external evaluation of their Named Person schemes via a Secondee from the Trustee Savings Bank.

Showing ones worth to the LEA will be important for continued funding, and being seen as a vital part of an LEA's work particularly in feeding back the parent perspective. Many schemes will need to focus more attention on this, in the final year.

Life after GEST

Generally it seems that schemes have gone through a metamorphosis, a period of rapid change where PPOs from a wide variety of backgrounds, experience and bases, with a wide variety of job descriptions, pay and conditions of work have been on a steep learning curve. The competing priorities between development work and direct case work has been a challenge to most schemes. The dissemination of practice via regional parent partnership group meetings, local and national conferences and more recently the National Parent Partnership Network has enabled LEAs to hear, learn and benefit from other innovative practice that was in place before the advent of Parent Partnership Schemes as well as that which has developed further with them. The range of activities undertaken and change taking place within many LEAs are forming strong foundations for a new era in parent partnership.

At the beginning some schemes envisaged their role developing so that at the end they would be redundant, as all LEA officers would take on the responsibility for full involvement of parents. However, given the competing demands on LEA officers, time needs to be protected to focus on parent partnership work, to follow up and monitor what is happening, to develop and evaluate approaches, to keep the momentum going and keep the LEA informed of up-to-the-minute research. Evaluation of the benefits schemes bring to their local communities will play a large part in determining whether they continue and can fulfil these needs.

It is heartening to note that some schemes are already written into the long-term development plans of their LEAs. Unfortunately the degree to which the government now controls the spending level of most councils and the competing demands there are on their budgets means that there is no guarantee that these development plans can be put into practice with appropriate resources. In addition future GEST money is specifically targeted at schools. Many schemes are not yet in a position to provide services needed to benefit from this funding (see section on schools). Different schemes are pursuing funding through a variety of avenues, including single regeneration budgets, city challenge, charitable trust status and so forth. In addition there are umbrella organisations for parents with special educational needs that are now set up as charities which will take over some of the functions of support groups and roles of befrienders, information disseminators, etc. There is also scope for schemes to develop across LEAs to use funding more efficiently, for example, by joint arrangements for training and assessment of volunteers.

Meanwhile the DFEE has commissioned a research project under the direction of Sheila Wolfendale at the University of East London which aims to evaluate the effectiveness of the GEST-funded Parent Partnership Schemes and to make recommendations about how parent partnership schemes can be sustained. This research will be completed in May 1997 and will report after that date. Until such time as this research project reports the preceding thoughts have been offered for the possible future directions of schemes and their life after GEST.

A final word

Most would agree that parents have the right to express their needs and wants from their own perspective and to be listened to. Parents who are dependent on services are further disadvantaged if they are not listened to by people with power. Self-advocacy and empowerment are the aims of many Parent Partnerships Schemes and should be inherent in the values and purposes of education.

Notes

The information for this chapter has been compiled from:

1 Anna Conrad's MSc dissertation, 'Parent Partnership Myth or Reality: An exploratory study into the scope and parameters of the GEST funded Parent Partnership schemes 1994–5' Psychology Department University of East London. This included the results of the questionnaire sent to the 110 LEAs (response rate 70 per cent), semi-structured interviews and a focus group interview of eleven.
2 The DFEE files for all the three years of the GEST bids and their sampling of LEAs development of Named Persons schemes in Jan/Feb 1996.
3 The database of the National Parent Partnership Network which was set up by the Council for Disabled Children in 1995–6 funded by DFEE grant.
4 Various studies /reports referred to in the text.
5 The work in the field of Teresa Furze, Senior Project Consultant, Senjit Parent Partnership Consortium (SENJIT stands for Special Educational Needs Joint Initiative for Training. It is based at the Institute of Education, University of London).

References

Advisory Centre for Education (1996) 'Travel Cost, Stranded or Resting in a Lay-by', Bulletin no. 70.

MENCAP (1995) 'An Investigation into the Implication of the Code of Practice Requirement to Identify a Named Person'. Royal Society for Mentally Handicapped Children and Adults.

OFSTED (1996) *The Implementation of the Code of Practice*. A report from the office of Her Majesty's Chief Inspector of Schools. London: HMSO.

Scottish Befriending Development Forum, 'Lets Befriend: a befriending resources

pack'. Victoria Centre, 102 Thornhill Road, Falkirk.
SENJIT (1995) 'Developing the Role of the Named Officer' Conference notes Senjit Parent Partnership Consortium, University of London Institute of Education.

8 Promoting the effective practice of partnership

Sheila Trier

Introduction

This chapter is written in acknowledgement of the work undertaken by all those involved in Parent Partnership Projects since April 1994. Many of the experiences and the issues that arose through this project's development may prove similar to the experiences of colleagues across the country. Achievements in Devon have been aided from the inception of the project by the full support, encouragement and commitment to the principles of partnership with parents from senior officers within the LEA. Without this level of support the work undertaken could not have been attained. The working style of the project has been strongly influenced by the belief that the quality of the partnership, which the project could build both with and for parents of children with special educational needs, would be most effective if close links were enjoyed with both voluntary and statutory agencies. As a result the contacts made during the life of the project have been many and varied. The contribution made by all who have actively supported the principles of open communication and ease of access to information for parents has been, and continues to be, highly valued but by far the most important contributions have been made by Devon parents.

The context

Devon is, physically, the third largest shire authority in England and Wales. It has a population of approximately one million, with considerable demographic diversity. This population distribution has had an impact on the work, and created some additional challenges, which will be described later on.

The LEA is organised from a central base with four area education offices in the north, east, south and west of the County, which provide support to the schools in each area and co-ordinate information and services for parents and pupils. Each area office has a team responsible for the organisation and administration of special services, i.e. issues relating to special educational needs including the statutory assessment and Statement processes. This provides a degree of flexibility in ensuring that local needs can be responded to at a local level. There continues to be a degree of instability and uncertainty about local government reorganisation which has proposed the establishment of three authorities based on Plymouth, Torbay and a 'new' Devon.

Current figures indicate that 3.4 per cent of the school population are the subjects of Statements of special educational need. The LEA maintains a range of special schools and support centres based in mainstream schools which provide for pupils with more significant special educational needs. In line with the Code of Practice (1994), Devon pursues a policy of maximum integration, wherever possible. In essence what is offered by the LEA is a situation where parents have a continuum of provision available. However, in the more rural areas access to this continuum may be limited by time and distance factors.

For many years the LEA has recognised that parents of young children with identified special educational needs require access to information and support. It offers a well-established Pre-school Advisory Service. In more recent years a Portage service has been developed in each area of the county. Additionally an annual residential weekend is organised for parents of Early Years children with SEN. The theme varies each year. The LEA has actively encouraged relationships with the voluntary organisations represented in the county.

Starting points

This GEST-funded Parent Partnership Scheme was the result of considerable discussion between SEN officers and advisers in conjunction with Community and Family Education in Devon. This valuable combination of perspectives proposed an initial strategy which incorporated a six-month research phase, designed to provide the project with immediate evidence of parents' perceptions of the strengths and weaknesses of the existing statutory assessment procedures. The original proposal saw this as the foundation for a second phase in which a 'Family Mentor' scheme was to be established for families involved in the assessment process. The research targeted one area of the county and would be used to inform the development of a county-wide working model.

The aims of the bid, perhaps typical of many projects in reflecting the DFE scheme objectives, were to:

1. encourage parental partnership;
2. ensure that parents feel they have been fully consulted and their views taken into consideration when the LEA assesses and makes a Statement in respect of their child's special educational needs;
3. contribute to the implementation of new procedures in the light of the 1993 Education Act Code of Practice;
4. support schools in the development of a proactive approach to promoting and publicising their provision.

The second objective was reworded from the original DFE scheme objective – 'To minimise both the conflict and the number of statutory appeals over the LEA processes of identifying, assessing and making statements for pupils with special educational needs' – as the new wording placed a greater emphasis on the principle of open dialogue between all parties which in itself could preempt the need for some parents to enter the appeal process.

I was appointed as project co-ordinator in March 1994, to take up the post in September. This intervening period was useful for my own planning and thinking especially as some rapid change to the original plan for the project became necessary.

The final version of the Code of Practice, issued in June 1994, included the Named Person role. Although not dissimilar to the concept of the 'Family Mentor', this late entry was particularly significant in that all LEA's were expected to have regard to the Code of Practice from September 1994. Devon's need for a county-wide response to the 'Named Person' requirement precluded the development of a pilot scheme.

Phase One – The listening process

The process of hearing parents' views was introduced through a county-wide consultation period. The purpose of this was to:

- make the aims of the project known to parents;
- hear parents' concerns about the strengths and weaknesses of the system to inform the more formal research;
- enable parents to become active partners in the development of the project;
- learn about the range of support systems already available to parents within the county;
- learn about the structure and support offered by other organisations to their volunteers.

It was essential that contact was made with parents as quickly as possible. There were two obvious routes for doing this, through voluntary organisations and schools. Both avenues were followed. The Disability Information and Advice Centres together with the Guild for Community Service were invaluable in providing information about voluntary organisations that updated and supplemented the initial information available to us. (They have also been excellent in giving guidelines and helpful advice about establishing and supporting a volunteer service.)

All voluntary organisations and parent support groups were invited to attend an initial meeting, with any parents who might be interested. This was a valuable and well-attended meeting which allowed for the sharing of information and concerns. One message related to concerns on the part of the voluntary organisations that they were not in a position, either in terms of time or resources, to take on the Named Person role (ACE 1994).

Schools were asked to inform parents about open meetings across the county. This strategy had the clear advantage of keeping schools informed about project activities at a point in time when they were heavily involved in planning their own school policies in response to the Code. The response from parents to these open meetings was remarkable. Surprise at the larger numbers than anticipated was expressed. One parent was later overheard to say 'I don't know why they're surprised. It's the first time anyone has ever asked me what I think about it all.'

These higher numbers also influenced the style of the meetings. As an opportunity to hear a range of parents' views about the identification and assessment procedures they were extremely effective. Parents seemed to welcome the greater clarity offered by the Code of Practice. Issues about resources were raised at all these meetings. Careful explanations were needed to clarify that issues about the actual funding were not part of the project's brief but that parents could be helped to understand how provision for their children might be made. Another concern raised related to the 'independence' of the project, since it was in part LEA funded and managed. There have been clear advantages from being so closely linked to the LEA, in terms of establishing good communication channels through this early development phase, which have offset the occasional disquiet created by the lack of independence.

These consultation meetings also served the purpose of highlighting how little information was readily available to parents about the early stages of identification and assessment, referred to in the Code as Stages One to Three. A range of issues relating to parents' perceptions of:

- the system as being unclear and unresponsive to both the needs of children and their parents,
- a sense of being seen as a 'nuisance', 'pushy' or that 'until you have a Statement you don't count',

suggested that the concerns of this group of parents were just as valid as those of parents whose children were subject to statutory assessment and statements. This has continued to influence subsequent developments for the project.

Varying degrees of scepticism relating to the insecurity of funding for the project and its links to the LEA were expressed at this time but a majority of parents indicated an interest in staying in touch with developments.

On reflection, this period of time was both very exciting and yet slightly daunting. Parents were being asked to contribute to the development of a concept which had nothing tangible to show. An act of faith was required. It was extremely reassuring to be able to make links with other projects in the south west through the regional network. Being able to share experiences and developments and offer mutual support, particularly in these early days, was – and still is – of great value. A major benefit in the southwest was the inclusion in the meetings of Supportive Parents for Special

Children, a parent-led group from Avon (before local government re-organisation) which had been in existence for approximately five years prior to the introduction of Parent Partnership Schemes. The model of working with parents developed by them has had a significant influence on the shape of this project (Broomhead and Darley 1992, Chapter 3 this volume).

One of the first steps taken before the project was established had been the development of a steering group. This had three parent members. It was recognised during the first term that not only were more parents required on this steering group but that with the county focus it would be helpful to have a steering group in each of the four areas. A model comprising equal numbers of parents, who might also be able to offer links to other groups, and professionals (to include health and social services) was developed with a useful working size suggestion of twelve in total. It was envisaged that these groups would be the key to a clear communication structure between parents and the LEA. The need to advance this, together with the confirmation of the funding for 1995–96, led to a second round of meetings with parents across the county. These meetings were very different in size and tone to the first meetings. Parents' suggestions regarding project developments were extremely helpful. The proposed model for the steering groups was adapted by each area to meet their own requirements. The steering groups play an extremely important role in focusing the work and guiding developments within their own area of Devon.

Formal research

The aims of the initial study were to explore the views of Devon parents about the statutory assessment procedures that may lead to a Statement of special educational needs being made with regard to a child. To this end the key research question to be asked was:

> What are the views of parents who have children with special educational needs on the Local Education Authority's identification and assessment procedures?

This was achieved by developing a tiered system of data collection (see Table 8.1).

1. The consultation phase, as described, with members of voluntary organisations and parents, which acted as a springboard to generate a broad understanding of parents' perspectives.

2. Postal questionnaire – a questionnaire was developed based on the issues raised by parents through the consultation process. This was sent to 114 parents, who had been through the assessment procedures for their child in the three years up to September 1994 (i.e. when the Code of Practice was introduced), in four cluster groups of schools in west Devon. These particular cluster groups were selected to reflect a range of

geographic and socio-economic conditions found within the county, from rural isolation to inner city settings with their associated issues.

3 A guided interview format – this was developed with open-ended questions designed to encourage parents to talk freely. It was intended to be carried out with eight parents selected from each cluster group to consider a variety of children's SEN. The interview was planned at this point to add flesh to the bones and pick up issues raised by the postal questionnaire.

Table 8.1 Data gathering

	Postal Questionnaires		**Interviews**	
	Sent out	**Returned**	**Requested**	**Completed**
Cluster group 1	19	9	8	8
Cluster group 2	39	30	8	8
Cluster group 3	18	13	8	3
Cluster group 4	37	27	8	7
Total	113	79	32	26
As percentage		69.9%		81.25%

Research findings

A wealth of information was gathered through this process. A formal presentation based on the key issues identified through this questionnaire and relevant to the work of the project was made in September 1995 to a composite audience of LEA professionals and parents. This was a deliberate move to ensure that the findings were equally available to all groups and individuals. Everyone invited received a copy of the proceedings even if they were unable to attend.

The issues covered are very similar to those raised in other studies (Adams 1986, Sandow *et al.* 1987, Bennett and Cass 1989, McCarthy 1991, Audit Commission 1992) and relate to the following

Quality of information

A clear written explanation for parents about the identification and assessment system was not readily available to parents at this point in time. Many parents indicated that they first heard about the statutory assessment process orally from a professional.

As Figure 8.1 indicates, the majority of parents considered this to be at least satisfactory, if not good. A few considered that it was poor. Additional comments, even from some parents who thought it was good, suggested that they would have liked to have had access to this information at an earlier point in time. The first written information which parents received was from the LEA at the start of the statutory assessment process. This has been criticised for being very formal in view of the legal elements involved. Figure 8.1 shows a greater proportion of parents indicating that it was poor. Parents are also sent guidance notes for their contribution to the assessment. A similar pattern can be seen with regard to this information.

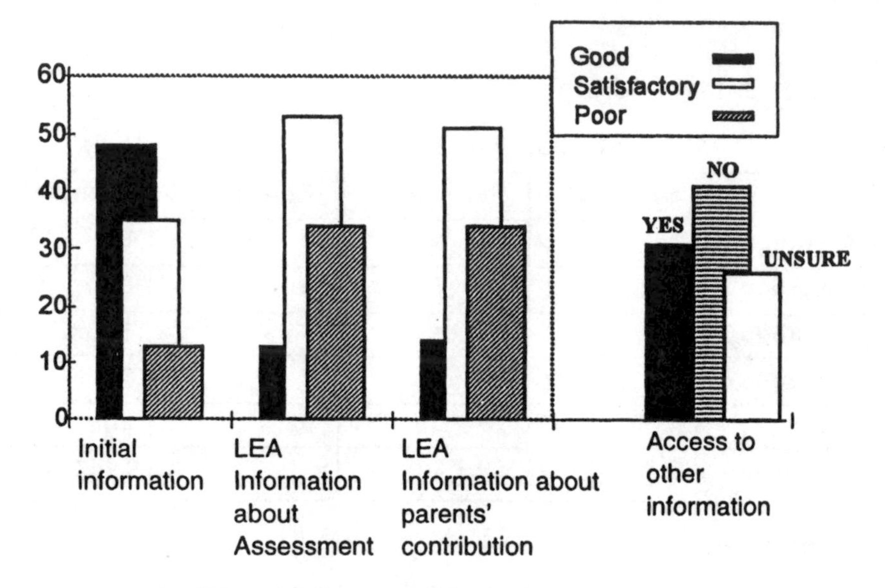

Figure 8.1 Quality of information given to parents

Parents were also asked whether they had sought further information from other sources. Data from the interviews suggests that these parents mainly sought more information from schools or from voluntary organisations. Another group of parents indicated that, although they would have liked to find out more, they were uncertain as to who or where to ask.

Involvement

The topic of how parents were involved through the process was considered in a number of ways. Information was gathered about:

- The parents' written contribution – this evidence indicated that 32 per cent of parents did not make a written response to the LEA giving their views about their child's need. Twelve per cent said they would have liked to but were not sure what to say.
- Report sharing – parents were questioned about whether the professionals involved in their child's assessment had provided an opportunity to

talk their advice with them. Some 41 per cent of parents would have liked more opportunities for discussion with professionals.

- Discussion of Statement – parents were asked if they had discussed the proposed Statement with anyone else. The information showed that more than 50 per cent of parents did discuss it with at least one other person. More parents shared this with a member of staff at their child's school than with any other group. Information from the interviews indicated that where parents feel confident that the school has their child's best interest at heart they turn to the school as a first move.
- Contact with the area education office – a majority of parents indicated that they had felt no need to make contact with the area office. Of the 27 per cent of parents who had made contact with the office most felt that this had been satisfactory, with only 10 per cent indicating that they were dissatisfied with the outcome. Another 15 per cent of parents said that they would have liked to make contact but felt uncertain or unsure about making this approach. It is in this situation that the parents' relationship with the school becomes of paramount importance. Where parents have confidence, trust and feel supported by the school there seems to be less likelihood of them needing to make direct contact with the office, even when they have extreme worries. 'I think the head had something to do with that [allocation of additional support], I think he pushed for it ... Well, I said, "I'll leave it to you because if I do it, I will get awful tongue twisted in doing it"'.

  On the other hand there are parents who do not have this level of trust. One, who had an unhappy experience with her child's previous school, commented, 'It is not just about the teacher having the knowledge and skills, they must have an interest in helping you and your child'.

Parents' feelings

Through the consultation process and the interviews a number of parents indicated an expectation that they would need to 'fight' to ensure that their child's needs were met. This impression had been picked up from the media or other parent contacts. None had actually found themselves in that position with their child. One father said, 'Not only was there no need to fight, the Education were ahead of us and offered support to the school before the Statement was ready so that J. could start at the right time.'

One of the themes that emerged on a frequent basis in interviews was that of the parents' dilemma between being seen as 'difficult', 'demanding', 'over anxious' and their concerns that their child's needs should be met appropriately.

It is not unexpected that parents experience very mixed feelings about the whole process. Terms that were used by parents during the consultation process were included in the questionnaire. Most parents responded to more than one category. So, for example, parents who said that they felt comfortable or involved in the process might also say that they felt stressed. Only three parents used all positive terms in their responses.

Independent support and advice

The response to the final question regarding the needs of parents for independent support and advice through the statutory assessment process was critical to the development of the Named Person requirement of the Code of Practice.

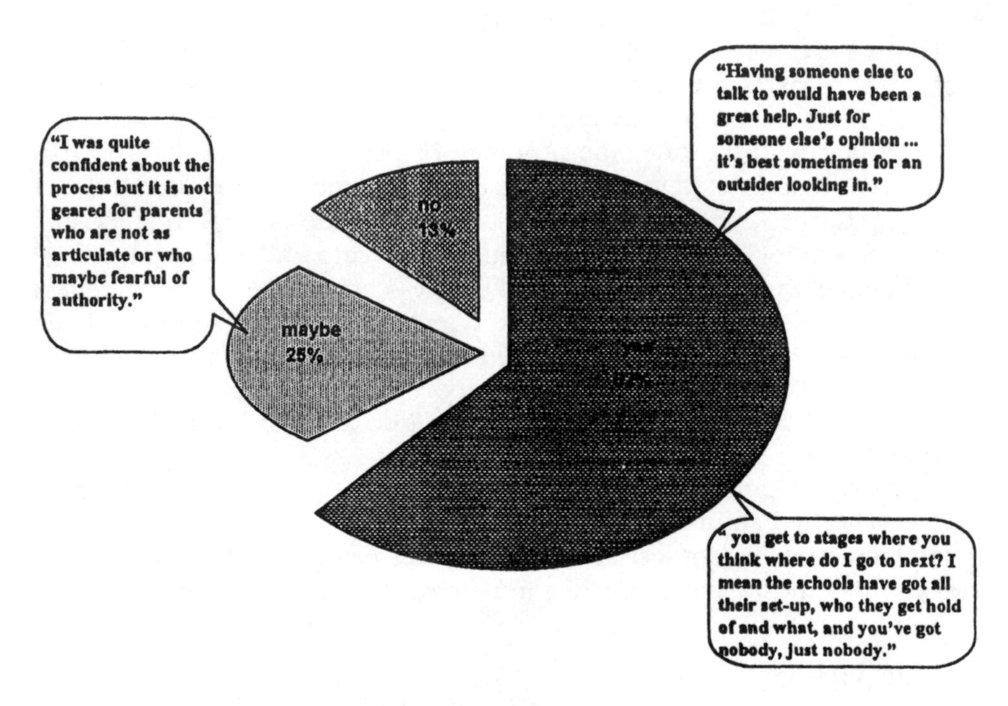

Figure 8.2 Independent advice and support

Figure 2 shows the very positive response to the concept of independent advice and support being available to parents. In the interviews parents also generally supported this idea. Some indicated that they would prefer the idea of support coming from a group situation rather than an individual contact. Parents also indicated that they would value support from another parent who could empathise with their situation. A few parents did not feel it to be necessary. They considered that they had been well supported by professionals through the whole process. This supports other evidence (Holland 1996) as this group were mainly parents of children with significant sensory and cognitive difficulties who had been identified at a very early age and had received a high degree of professional support through the preschool years.

The influence of these research findings has had a significant effect on partnership arrangements within the LEA. This information provides a focal point and perspective which has furthered the manner in which the LEA views relationships with parents.

Phase Two – Finding solutions

The timing for the appointment of the project workers in each area of Devon marked a period of intense development activity. They needed to assimilate much information very quickly. A rapid learning curve was experienced by all! Their role is essentially that of a community worker. They are not case workers or Named Persons, although the LEA does ensure that parents who do not identify anyone for that role are given their names as a contact point when the final Statement is issued.

Immediate action relating to key points from the research was taken with two central themes:

- a response to the duty to ensure that parents could access independent support and advice;
- to ensure that relevant information about identification and assessment procedures was readily available for all parents.

The advent of Special Partners

Throughout the first phase the issues involved for all parties in establishing a Named Person scheme were under constant review (Kerr *et al.* 1994, Robinson 1995, Westerman 1995). It became clear that the role would need to be re-defined to take into account the implications for parents whose children were identified as being at Stages One to Three in the Code, as recognised through the consultation process. The basic question related to who should decide how much information and support a parent might require at a given point in time. There could only be one answer to this: the parent concerned. Working from the same principles as the Code of Practice in recognising a continuum of needs, it was considered that support should be available to parents whose child may be at any of the assessment stages. This approach was also based on the concept that parents who had access to accurate information and support from an early point in time would feel more confident that their views regarding their child's needs had been actively heard. The decision to rename the role resulted from a need to reflect its broader nature. The selected title of Special Partner was the outcome of much discussion with a range of parents and professionals.

The Special Partner in Devon is essentially a befriending, empowering role. It seemed that this approach could offer a greater degree of flexibility, both for those who volunteer to provide this support as well as for parents who request support. As befrienders Special Partners are not in a position to offer specialised advice. They do know who parents can turn to for this and actively encourage this when required. They are in a strong position to ensure that parents have access to quality information. It is anticipated that this broader, more flexible approach will ensure a model of good working practice which is responsive to the clearly expressed needs of parents.

A scheme of this nature is totally dependent upon the willingness of volunteers to work within it. It is seen as essential that they should feel valued for their efforts. A support model comprising of an initial training programme followed by regular meetings, which could also provide further training opportunities, was considered fundamental for volunteers to feel confident with the role. The initial training comprises a ten session course which covers topics relating to the role of the befriender and confidentiality as well as ensuring a working knowledge of the requirements of the Code of Practice and how this is implemented at a local level. Accreditation for this course under the Devon parent education programme is currently in hand. It is not anticipated that all Special Partners will wish to follow the accredited route. This move is to ensure that those who wish to use the programme as evidence of personal learning have opportunities to do so.

Recruitment of Special Partners across the county has generally not been a problem except in one particular area. In fact a greater problem has been in ensuring that the delivery of the initial training is accessible to all those interested. The Devon team has trained 60 Special Partners over three residential weekends. The development of a group identity among the volunteers was one clear benefit of this initial approach. There were two major disadvantages to delivering the training in this way. Firstly, it made for a very intensive programme. More importantly, some potential volunteers had family commitments which precluded them from attending. The project workers have now undertaken the City and Guilds 730 Further and Adult Education Teacher's Certificate which allows them to act as course leaders. This has aided the recent development of local training courses, delivered on a sessional basis.

All volunteers are expected to attend this initial training regardless of their previous background. It forms an essential part of the selection process and allows both volunteers and trainers opportunities to resolve misconceptions about the nature of the work involved. This dialogue is also helpful in establishing individual volunteers' strengths and interests which facilitates agreement about the nature of their commitment to the network. The protection of vulnerable clients is a prime consideration but the scheme must also protect itself from the possibility of any legal consequences which might result from careless acceptance procedures.

While parents are the prime source of volunteers (Gascoigne 1995), the role has also appealed to others e.g. members of voluntary organisations, retired teachers, social workers, etc.

There are certain costs involved without which the scheme cannot operate. Public, employers and professional liability insurance is provided for volunteers. Travel expenses can be reclaimed and BT chargecards are issued to avoid difficulties in claiming telephone expenses. In exceptional circumstances additional child-minding expenses, incurred on account of essential activities, have been paid. The costs of all these have been covered by the project.

To date the drop-out rate has been minimal. Approximately six volunteers decided through the training that they were not yet ready to support other parents. Another six have stepped down on a temporary basis due to their own circumstances. It is important to maintain flexibility for volunteers, given the nature of the work involved.

In the first nine months of this scheme over 100 parents have been supported by a volunteer. Sixty per cent of these parents were involved in the statutory assessment proceedings. Twenty per cent had children for whom Statements were already in existence. The final group of parents have children whose SEN have been identified by the school.

An evaluation of the work undertaken by Special Partners is currently in hand. This will consider the role from the perspective of the parent, the special partner and other professionals (where they have been involved). One observation regarding the value of the role is that quite a number of the volunteers use each other for support when they need to attend review meetings or go through paperwork regarding their own children.

Access to information

The second priority was to develop, in consultation with steering group members and other professionals, information packs and later audio-cassette tapes. These are now available to parents through schools, advisory support teams and area offices. The initial response to these has been very positive but, as with any new development, it is essential to ensure that the information this contains is accessible and helpful to parents in understanding how the system works.

A newsletter, 'Devon Connections', has been produced. This actively promotes the range of partnerships available to parents in Devon and draws on the good practice to be found in different settings across the county.

The arrival of the project workers also facilitated the setting up of local contact points for parents. A leaflet outlining the work of the project and promoting the supportive nature of the work with parents was widely distributed. Although not a Helpline in the accepted sense of the word, project workers are regularly and increasingly contacted by parents. Almost 200 enquiries were received during the first twelve months. The figures indicate that approximately one-third of the calls they receive are general requests for information and reassurance usually related to pre-statutory assessment issues.

There were two key groups who needed to be kept informed about developments through this period. Finding an appropriate mechanism to ensure regular communication with all the voluntary organisations has proved difficult. Devon Voluntary Agencies Forum was identified as providing a good contact point. Regrettably the application to join was denied because, although providing a volunteer service, technically the project is not a voluntary group. The project continues to welcome involvement with voluntary agencies and a considerable number of Special Partners have strong connections with them.

As the Special Partner network is intended to complement the advice and support already available to many parents through their schools, it was important to keep them informed about developments. The long-term goal is a pool of Special Partners in each local cluster of schools, providing a local network of support for parents with established links to local schools and other professionals within the area. A letter was sent to all schools in the county explaining the development. The project workers actively sought invitations to the cluster group meetings to build links in the areas and to clarify any potential misunderstandings. Generally speaking they received a very warm welcome from these groups of headteachers. They also made contact with a wide range of other professionals including SENCOs, advisory support teams, area education office staff, EWOs, school nurses and social workers, to name but a few! These links have proved invaluable as the project gathers momentum. Increasingly parents are being encouraged to make contact with the project through one of the professionals already involved with their child. Schools have responded with a degree of variability. Some have welcomed input in developing parent support groups and have actively encouraged parents to participate in the Special Partner training. Others have supported teachers in attending a one-day training session run by the project. This day course offers teachers the opportunity to reflect and share ideas about their existing practice with pa ents and has been very positively received.

The principle of making information readily available and accessible for a wide group of parents has also been promoted through 'Special Needs Awareness Days' which have been held in each area of the county. These are essentially open days with displays provided by a wide range of groups including the area education office, all the advisory support teams, mainstream and special schools, community and further education teams, voluntary organisations as well as health and social services representatives. The response to each has proved their worth.

Within Devon there are two distinct groups of parents who provide a continuing challenge. Both groups should be recognised as being distinctly disadvantaged in accessing information and support. The first group are parents who live in isolated rural locations. There is some evidence to suggest that these families tend to have 'strong traditions of self-reliance'. (Halliday 1995). Often their links with schools may be tenuous because their children are 'bussed' in. Additionally small village primary schools may only have the one child with a Statement which can leave the parents feeling even more distant. In one area of Devon where the recruitment of Special Partners has been slower the project has focused its energies on developing parent support groups not based on schools but across a wider community. These are beginning to develop identities of their own. Special Partner training is available to lead parents in such groups. Another area has made the decision to focus on parents of preschool children with identified special needs with a 'drop-in' being held once a month at the local Child Development Centre.

The second group of parents are those for whom the education system has always been a source of alienation (Galloway *et al.* 1994). Experience to date suggests that the most effective strategy for this group is based on the principle of personal recommendation through contacts in the community. For this reason close links with schools and other community-based agencies are being developed in inner-city areas.

> the Parent Partnership Schemes are emerging as a very powerful and very positive voice for parent partnership, but it is still quite early days and I think we need to learn a lot about working with all parents and not with those parents who are already active in a voluntary organisation and able to access their own advice. (Russell 1996)

Into the future...

This has been a fast-moving project with a wide range of developments on a broad front. The work currently in hand must be consolidated before the end of the GEST-funded period. It has been overtly stated, from a very early point in the planning of this project, that the goal at the end of this formal funding time would be to establish an organisation that is freestanding of the LEA. An active awareness of this by participating parents and professionals has been advanced at appropriate opportunities. This goal now begins to loom large. The 'exit strategy' process was, in effect, started last November with the submission of a paper to the Education Committee. This outlined the nature of the project and drew the attention of Members to the statutory duty placed on the LEA to ensure access for parents to independent support and advice through and beyond the statutory assessment and Statement processes.

A review of the current steering group structures and arrangements has recently been completed. This activity incorporated opportunities for all involved with the steering groups to express their preferred options for the future. The majority of responses have indicated that the steering groups would like to maintain and develop the range of activities currently being undertaken by the project. There is a recognition that the project workers are essential to the ongoing co-ordination and support of the Special Partner network but considerable concerns have been expressed regarding the uncertainty of funding. A key task over the next few months is to find assured funding routes.

A further complication is the uncertainty about the development of the three new authorities. One of the suggestions made by group members was to constitute three different groups to reflect the changing face of the LEA. A majority decision has been made in favour of retaining the current structure of area groups but with representatives from these forming a county group to move the project into a voluntary organisation in its own right. The advantages expressed by group members in favour of this option indicated that this would provide the new group with a degree of consistency and stability over the transition period. Other comments referred to the concept of there being a strength in numbers. Advantages relating to the maintenance of quality training and support for the Special Partner network were also highlighted. The next step is to convene a meeting of the proposed county group to develop an identity, philosophy and constitution for the emerging organisation.

The future uncertainties create a challenge. How many project officers/co-ordinators have previous experience of effecting a transfer of this nature? One piece of valuable advice offered has been to think forward and ask not what should be happening in twelve months, but in two or even three years time! The principles of partnership in terms of rights, equality, reciprocity and, in particular, empowerment will continue to shape developments to ensure 'that the parental voice is heard and has influence' (Wolfendale 1992). We believe that a flourishing parent-led organisation, which holds a mutually beneficial working relationship with both the LEA and other voluntary organisations, is a clear and achievable goal.

References

ACE (1994) 'Partners or Poodles?', *ACE Bulletin*, 60, July/August, p.1.

Adams, F. (Ed.) (1986) *Special Education*. Essex: Longman.

Audit Commission (1992) *Getting in on the Act*. London: HMSO.

Bennett, N. and Cass, A. (1989) *From Special to Ordinary Schools: case studies in integration*. London: Cassell Educational.

Broomhead, R. and Darley, P. (1992) 'SPSC: working towards partnership in Avon' in Booth, T., Swann, W., Masterton, M. and Potts, P. (Eds) *Policies for Diversity in Education*. London and New York: Routledge.

Devon LEA (1995/96) *Devon Connections* (Newsletter) Issue nos. 1 and 2 September 1995, January 1996. Torquay: Devon Learning Resources.

Devon LEA (1995) *Understanding Special Educational Needs in the 1993 Education Act: a straightforward guide for parents and carers in Devon*. Torquay: Devon Learning Resources.

DFE (1994) *Code of Practice on the Identification and Assessment of Special Educational Needs*. London: HMSO.

Galloway, D., Armstrong, D. and Tomlinson, S. (1994) *The Assessment of Special Educational Needs: whose problem?* London: Longman.

Gascoigne, E. (1995) *Working with Parents as Partners in SEN*. London: David Fulton Publishers.

Halliday, J. (1995) *Children's Services and Care in Rural Devon*. Devon County Council, Department of Social Services and Education, County Hall, Exeter.

Holland, S. (1996) 'The Special Needs of Parents', *Educational Psychology in Practice*, 12, 1, pp. 24–30.

Kerr, L., Sutherland, L. and Wilson, J. (1994) *A Special Partnership: a practical guide for Named Persons and parents of children with special educational needs*, Children in Scotland. London: HMSO.

McCarthy, T. (1991) 'Children with Special Educational Needs: parents' knowledge of procedures and provisions', *British Journal of Special Education*, 18, 1, Research Supplement, pp.17–19.

Robinson, J. (1995) Feasibility Study into whether SCOPE in the West Region can set up or participate in setting up a Quality Service providing a Network of Named Persons' to the Parents of Children with CP being Statemented under the 1993 Education Act. Internal Report to SCOPE, Pamwell House, 160 Pennywell Road, Easton, Bristol, BS5 0TX.

Russell, P. (1996) Witness evidence in House of Commons Education Committee, Second Report, Special Educational Needs: The Working of the Code of Practice and the Tribunal. London: HMSO.

Sandow, S., Stafford, D. and Stafford, P. (1987) *An Agreed Understanding? Parent–professional communication and the 1981 Education Act.* Windsor: NFER-Nelson.

Westerman, I. (1995) 'An Investigation into the Implementation of the Code of Practice Requirement to Identify a "Named Person"'. Report on behalf of MENCAP, 117–23 Golden Lane, London, EC1Y 0RT.

Wolfendale, S. (1992) *Empowering Parents and Teachers: working for children.* London: Cassell.

9 Supporting parents at the Special Educational Needs Tribunal

Katy Simmons

The Tribunal in context

The 1993 Education Act created a new framework for the provision of special education. However, the Act created not only the Code of Practice with its emphasis on partnership with parents, but also the Special Educational Needs Tribunal to which parents might turn when partnership had failed. Even before the Tribunals had begun work, there were widely differing views on whether the new legislation would increase partnership or lead to increased conflict. The Department for Education at the time claimed that the number of parents making appeals against LEA decisions would not increase. The voluntary sector and the legal profession took a different view and braced themselves for 'a boom in business' (*TES*, 25 February 1994). Which of these two views has proved correct is only now beginning to emerge. The *Guardian* reported in 1994 that 'the hope is that the existence of the new tribunals will sharpen up LEA practice and eventually, once the backlog of the old system has been worked through, keep appeals to a minimum.' (*Guardian*, 1 March). We are now beginning to see whether this hope has been fulfilled.

This chapter will look at the impact of the Special Educational Needs Tribunal on a system that in other areas holds partnership as its goal. It will look in particular at the impact on parents of the tribunal system and at the new needs that have been created, particularly for parent representation. It will also look at the implications for professionals of the new appeal system. Professionals are urged by the Code to work in partnership with parents; is such partnership possible when professionals are likely to be called as witnesses at hearings, or put on oath when giving evidence about a child's needs?

Creating the Tribunal

The Special Educational Needs Tribunal was created under section 177 of the 1993 Education Act and along with the rest of the Act, came into being on 1 September 1994. It replaced a discredited local appeal system which, as part of the 1981 Education Act, had long been a cause of complaint from parents and from the voluntary sector.

Under the new Act, for the first time, parents who disagreed with decisions made by their LEA had rights of appeal to an independent body. The Tribunal functioned under the direct supervision of the council on Tribunals and its decisions would be binding. The president of the new Tribunal was appointed directly by the Lord Chancellor as was the panel of Tribunal chairmen. The new Tribunal was invested with a number of powers, including that of ordering the discovery of documents, of requiring attendance and of administering oaths to witnesses. The number of opportunities for parents to appeal against LEA decisions was greatly increased.

The first annual report published by the Special Needs Tribunal in December 1995 recorded that by the end of its first year of work, it had received 1,170 appeals and that the steady rise in volume of appeals showed no sign of slowing down. The report stated that there was evidence that 'the number of appeals registered during the Tribunal's second year will be substantially greater than during the first year' (Annual Report, SEN Tribunal, 1995, p.8). LEAs which had been accustomed under the old system to very limited numbers of appeals were taken by surprise by the large numbers of parental challenges and by the beginning of 1996, strikingly different views were emerging from parents and from LEAs of both the operation and the impact of the new system. Further, it was becoming clear that although the new system had given parents new opportunities to challenge LEA decisions, it had created new needs. It was clear that the new system was being used most effectively by more confident and articulate parents: concerns were beginning to grow about how the appeal system might be made more accessible to the less confident.

The Select Committee

In March 1996, the House of Commons Education Committee published the results of its investigations into the working of the Code of Practice and the Tribunal. The evidence presented showed increasing polarisation between the views put forward by LEAs and those presented by voluntary organisations speaking on behalf of parents of children with special needs. However, in its report, the Committee chose not to become involved in the increasingly bitter areas of dispute being opened up as a result of Tribunal judgements.

Instead, in its report the Committee pointed to the general welcome that there had been for the establishment of the Tribunal. It then drew attention to preliminary evidence from research carried out by Dr Neville Harris at Liverpool University that showed that the overwhelming majority of parents expressed general satisfaction with the Tribunal.

However, the Committee was concerned that many parents had difficulty understanding the appeal procedures and drew attention to the need for support and advice for parents seeking to appeal. They also expressed concern that often parents were not able to obtain sufficient supporting evidence other than from the LEA against whose decision they were appealing. They pointed out how difficult it was for a parent to call an LEA employee as a witness; they commented 'Teachers and other LEA professionals called to give evidence to a Tribunal can be put in a difficult position' (Select Committee, p.viii).

Having considered a great deal of both oral and written evidence, the Committee made two specific recommendations:

1 that the president of the Tribunal should include in his written guidance to Tribunal chairmen advice on how they can enable befrienders to perform their role effectively;

2 that LEAs should ensure that wherever possible evidence at Tribunal hearings is presented by the LEA officers directly concerned with the child's assessment.

It is significant that the only two recommendations following the extensive consultation process focused on the need for evidence and parental need for support. Both areas have direct relevance to partnership with parents: they are likely to be ones that continue to be problematic as the work of the Tribunal develops.

Getting the evidence

The president of the Special Educational Needs Tribunal, Trevor Aldridge QC, made it clear from the outset that the remit of the Tribunal was not to consider history, but to look at the child's needs on the day of the hearing. Thus, there is at every hearing a heavy emphasis on evidence, and evidence of the most up-to-date kind. This emphasis has considerable implications for parents and for those advising parents.

LEAs have immediate and easy access to up-to-date evidence.They can, and often do, send their professionals into school the day before a hearing. Unfortunately, as the employers of most of the people who have the most regular contact with the child, they can, and, evidence suggests, in some LEA routinely do, exert an influence on the nature of the data that is collected.

The reluctance of LEA employees to attend as witnesses on behalf of parents was brought to the attention of the Select Committee. The British Dyslexia Association, for example, reported that 'School staff are usually very reluctant to attend hearings as witnesses for parents. They seem to regard this as speaking against the LEA, who have been known to tell teachers they cannot attend the Tribunal' (Select Committee, p.31).

Professionals may well have every intention of working co-operatively with parents but it would be naive to believe that they are always able to do so. The president of the Tribunal himself commented:

> In the spirit of parent partnership engendered by the Code of Practice I had thought that those most closely concerned with the child in question would have no hesitation on coming forward to offer their help. It turns out that in some cases local education authorities are reluctant that any of their employees, and this will particularly apply to teachers, should give evidence 'for' the parents and 'against' the authority. This takes a confrontational view of the appeal to the Tribunal which seems unfortunate. (Annual Report of the SEN Tribunal, p.14)

Recent research by IPSEA (the Independent Panel for Special Education Advice) has confirmed the extent of this problem (IPSEA 1996). In a study based on telephone interviews with 42 parents who had used IPSEA's Free Representation Service, accounts of witness intimidation featured regularly. Twenty-two of the parents interviewed had called as witnesses employees of the LEAs against whose decisions they were appealing. Of these, twelve parents had issued a summons to oblige them to attend. Only three parents reported that LEA employees had attended quite willingly. In some cases, sensitivity to the position of the people involved had actually prevented parents from calling the witness who would have been most useful to their case. Parents commented, 'We felt it was unfair to call anyone employed by the LEA because of possible recriminations' and 'We were going to ask our child's teacher but she declined after pressure from the LEA'.

Those who issued a summons to compel attendance did so to protect their witness. As one parent commented,'We issued a summons to our child's class teacher. Otherwise she wouldn't have attended. She was worried about recriminations'.

The fear of recriminations was not unfounded: one parent reported that they had issued a witness summons to the Special Needs Co-ordinator in their child's school and put her on oath. The SENCO had previously told the parents that she had been threatened by an LEA officer who said her job was at stake and told her she wouldn't find a job anywhere else. Another parent reported that 'Things were very awkward for the speech and language therapist. We know it has affected her career. She is shunned at meetings'.

This difficulty of calling witnesses presents parents with real problems. In many cases the professionals whose evidence is vital will be involved with the child for years to come. Parents often have to decide whether they will risk alienating the professional in the future by issuing a summons, or whether it is in the child's long-term interests to avoid the issue by not calling the professional at all, thereby weakening their case. In circumstances such as this, 'partnership' may take on a hollow ring. Such issues will have to be resolved if partnership is to develop in a meaningful way.

For parents who can afford it, the obvious solution to these problems is to seek an independent second opinion. But the cost of such independent evidence puts it beyond the means of most people and even for those who can afford it, appropriate evidence may be hard to find.

Available evidence

Such difficulties would not arise if the evidence already available to parents was written in the way that the law intends. One of the immediate results of the Tribunal's work has been to put professionals employed by the LEA into the spotlight, not just as potential witnesses but as advice givers who contribute in the course of assessment. What that advice should contain has, since the Tribunals began work, been a subject of some dispute between representatives of the LEAs and those representing parents of children with special needs.

This dispute was given public airing when the Select Committee took oral evidence in February 1996 and was exemplified in the exchange between Vincent McDonnell, principal education officer for Staffordshire, representing the Society of Education Officers and John Wright, Administrator of IPSEA. Speaking of the inadequacy of the advice before both LEAs and subsequently tribunals, John Wright pointed out that in some LEAs, professionals were being dissuaded from writing their professional opinion on the provision necessary to meet a child's needs, their brief being to stick to the description of the needs. He went on to claim that if professionals do not present their views on provision, then 'the LEA are not adequately briefed when they decide what provision is required ... and neither is the tribunal' (Select Committee, p.7). He commented that if the LEA's professional advice is full, as the Regulations actually say it should be, there ought not to be a need for independent professional advice.

The LEA view, as presented by Mr McDonnell was very different. He claimed that the role of the professional was not to comment on provision, but simply to identify need. In his opinion, professional advice givers are 'there to advise the local education authority ... who ... [has to] ... make best judgment about how we respond to those identified needs looking at the range of provision that is available' (Select Committee, p.8).

This public disagreement highlights the way in which the work of the Tribunal has brought aspects of the statementing process under close scrutiny. Given such disparity of views, it is important for professionals to be clear on what the law in this area says.

Following the law

Briefly, the law in this area can be summarised as follows: as part of the assessment process, the LEA must seek advice from a number of sources and has statutory duties relating to the nature of the Advice it collects. Regulation 6 (2) of the 1994 Education (Special Educational Needs) Regulations, sets out the statutory obligation of LEAs in relation to the contents of Advice. This Regulation gives clear emphasis, not only to the setting out of a child's needs, but also to the LEA's obligation to require the professional involved to comment on the provision that the child needs.

When drawing up the Statement, it will be the LEA which is required, under section 168 (2) (b) of the 1993 Education Act, to specify the special educational provision to be made for the child. The Code of Practice goes further (section 4:8) in saying that the provision should be quantified.

One might argue, like Mr McDonnell, that it is the LEA that has these duties, not the advice giver. However, without Advice that comments on provision, the LEA has only half the evidence that it is by law required to collect. Mr McDonnell is right to say that the Advice giver cannot determine provision. But the fact remains that LEAs cannot make proper decisions without having before them advice such as the Regulations prescribe.

The work of the Tribunal has put this area of the law into the spotlight. It is likely to remain a contentious area until the issue is resolved, for example by the issuing of a circular from the Department of Education and Employment setting out good practice or by the incorporation of guidelines into the Code of Practice. Until then, the issue of evidence remains a source of difficulty for parents and a source of dispute between LEAs and the voluntary sector. For partnership with parents to develop, then professionals will need to be clear about what evidence they are required to give: some may need support from their professional organisations if they are fully to fulfil the role that the law intends for them. Parents who are made aware of the legal requirements of the contents of professional Advice will find it difficult to work with and trust professionals, who, for whatever reason, are reluctant to give written advice which covers not only their child's needs but also the provision which they require.

Representation

The next main difficulty for parents is the presentation of their case and the hearing itself. When the Tribunals were set up, Trevor Aldridge said on a number of occasions that the process should be 'parent friendly'. Most parents speak positively of their experiences of the staff at the Tribunal: Neville Harris, for example, reported that 'Most parents found the tribunal staff were helpful and that the information they received on the tribunal and its procedure was generally clear and intelligible' (Select Committee, p.51).

However, the tribunal process is part of the judicial system and as such is intimidating and stressful even for articulate and confident parents. Only parents with the lowest of incomes are eligible for legal aid to prepare their case. There is no legal aid for representation at hearings and the average cost of solicitor representation is at least £1,000. There is, moreover, no evidence that representation by a solicitor is necessarily helpful for parents or in the interests of the child: Harris, himself a lawyer, puts the case that a possible increase in legal representation, supported by legal aid, might be helpful in more complex cases. He does, however, admit that such a development may lead to more legalistic hearings and consequently 'increased formality, confrontation and reduced parental participation' (Select Committee, p.52).

Parents who feel unable to represent themselves do not have many options if, as is the case for many, legal representation is not possible because of costs. The need is certainly there, as IPSEA's research demonstrated.

The likelihood that the tribunals would create a new need for parents to be represented was recognised well before the first hearing was held. Both the voluntary sector and representatives of solicitors' organisations were reported to be preparing for a great increase in appeals and for the need to give support and advice to parents (*TES*, 25 February 1994). Their concerns about the need for representation have proved to be well founded. The scale of the problem is seen in representations to the Select Committee. The submission from the Council for Disabled Children, for example, commented:

> Notwithstanding the commitment to informality, the tribunal is a potentially stressful and alarming event for parents. A number of parents have commented on the need to have guidance on contributing to and fully understanding the Tribunal proceedings ... There is growing evidence that they will also need information and support from trained advisers and advocates in order to collect, analyse and present their evidence.
> (Select Committee, p.39)

The first systematic account of parental perceptions of the new system, IPSEA's study, *Representing Parents at the Special Educational Needs Tribunal*, although a small study, highlighted the general concern felt by parents about how their case should be presented (IPSEA 1996). A number of parents expressed real difficulty with the process of appeal:

> 'We were overwhelmed.'
> 'I was terrified.'
> 'I couldn't have done it on my own. It's a very emotional and stressful time ... I couldn't think straight.'
> 'We felt totally confused by the whole system.'
> 'Without help, I wouldn't have gone through with it.'

Although the Tribunal set out to avoid being a forum for lawyers, parents found it essential to have guidance on the legal points underlying their case and spoke with relief of the volunteers who had helped them present their case.

> 'What I needed was legal expertise. They pointed me in the right direction.'
> 'He helped me sum up all the legal points and could quote chapter and verse. He proved the LEA wasn't working within the Code of Practice.'

The hearing, in particular, presented problems for parents and some found participation in a quasi-judicial process very daunting indeed. They needed not only support but also someone who would take over the whole process.

> 'I was terrified at the thought of the hearing. I would have stayed at home ... if I could.'

Parents varied in the kind of help they wanted and 'representation', as reflected in this study, ranged between supporting a parent in presenting their own case to acting as an advocate and putting the case on their behalf. Support did not end with the hearing – there was clearly a need for continued advice, especially when the appeal was lost. Some parents felt distressed and bemused by the whole process: as one parent said, 'Our argument at the hearing was so good and the LEA's case was so terrible that I still don't know why we lost'. In such a situation, there was an obvious need for discussion of what options remained open to the parent and what they might do next.

Non-implementation

The stressful nature of the hearing inevitably sets up a situation where the notion of partnership begins to wear thin. This situation is made worse when, as recent evidence suggests, even after a successful hearing the parent finds that 'nothing happens'. Evidence presented to the Select Committee gave examples of individual cases where, following a successful appeal, parents found that their LEA did not implement the Tribunal Order. IPSEA's research showed non-implementation of Orders to be a widespread problem. Although the Tribunal's Orders are legally binding and therefore enforceable by law, many parents found that once they had their judgement, nothing happened at all. Only two families interviewed by IPSEA reported that following the Tribunal, their LEA took swift action to implement the judgement. The IPSEA research showed that 'once the Tribunal decision has been given, matters appear to drift into an administrative no-man's land' (IPSEA, p.13). For many parents, the successful appeal to the Tribunal did not resolve their difficulties: it simply punctuated a continuing process of disagreement.

There is clear evidence that following Tribunal judgements in favour of the parents, LEAs deliberately 'go slow'. Amendment to the Regulations is necessary which would impose time limits on LEAs responding to judgements and Orders issued by the Tribunal. But until such an amendment is made to the Regulations, parents will continue to need advice and support long after the hearing.

Who will support parents?

There is agreement in the voluntary sector and among lawyers that parents need support and advice. However, opinion is divided on where this support should come from and undoubtedly this issue will continue to be an area of debate. Not surprisingly the legal profession has made a case for increased legal representation at Tribunals: both Neville Harris and the Education Law Association put forward the argument to the Select Committee that legal aid should be extended to cover representation. The Council for Disabled Children supports this view but also argues for the extension of the role of the parent partnership officer in order to 'act as interpreter, befriender and adviser and also to hear the views presented in order to better advise and support the parent if problems remain after the hearing. (Select Committee, p.40).

Both approaches could be seen as problematic. It is unlikely in the current climate of financial stringency, where legal aid is being cut across the board, that there is likely to be acceptance of the need for extending it. Following a recent High Court ruling which prevented parents from obtaining legal aid in their child's name to challenge Tribunal decisions, there was swift reaction from both the legal profession and the voluntary sector. However, those attempting to press the case for a change in legal aid rules to allow parental appeal on a point of law have so far been unsuccessful. The point was made again in a number of submissions to the Select Committee and was underlined by the Committee in their report. Despite the general awareness that the legal aid barrier disadvantages individual children and blocks the development of case law, there has been no sign of change. It is therefore unlikely that the case for further extension of legal aid would meet with success.

But developing the role of the parent partnership officer may be equally problematic. The problem is, simply, that parent partnership officers are not independent: they are employed by the local education authorities against whose decisions parents are appealing. Conflict of interest is a potentially insurmountable difficulty. Few parent partnership officers represent parents at Tribunal hearings and many are known to refer parents directly to the voluntary sector when it becomes clear that appeal is inevitable. It is not only the hearing that presents a problem: where, for example, following non implementation of a Tribunal Order, the best advice to a parent would be to take legal action, it is hard to imagine that a parent partnership officer, employed by the same LEA, could act in an unfettered way.

What of the voluntary sector? Can it cope with the potential volume of work that might come its way? Disappointingly, the voluntary sector has yet to take on the full implications of the tribunal system. As the Council for Disabled Children pointed out, 'representation requires more knowledge and skills than befriending' (Select Committee, p.39). Representation requires close attention to detail, understanding of the legal process and confidence necessary to engage in direct conflict with decision-makers. Not every one wants to do it. Further, there are issues of indemnity which are often difficult to resolve. Potential volunteers are well aware that often much is at stake at a tribunal hearing and that possible litigation could follow inadequate representation.Consequently, the voluntary sector has not rushed to meet the need. Some organisations, like the Royal National Institute for the Blind and ASBAH (Association for Spina Bifida and Hydrocephalus) already had an advocacy service and are developing that service to respond to the new needs created by the tribunals. But resources are limited and even with its existing structure, the RNIB has estimated that 80 per cent of its parents go unrepresented to the Tribunal (Select Committee, p.38).

If all parents are to gain access to the tribunals, then it is essential that representation is extended – only concerted action from the voluntary sector, or a radical review of the role and nature of the parent partnership officer's work, can begin to meet the need.

Without action?

If the need for representation is not addressed, then those parents challenging LEA decisions will undoubtedly remain an articulate and energetic minority, fuelling a growing mythology that the tribunals are in some vague sense 'unfair'. This view is expressed in an extreme way in the submission of Suffolk LEA to the Select Committee. Suffolk expressed concern about:

> the emergence of a two tier service for parents. Those who take advantage of the Tribunal system do tend to achieve extra resources for their children compared to those whose parents do not seek to by-pass LEA policies or criteria aimed at ensuring a fair allocation of finite resources to pupils with similar levels of educational need.
> (Select Committee, p.82)

While this submission is challengeable on a number of issues, it is correct, however, in pointing out that a two-tier system of Statements is emerging in many LEAs. In one group are those parents who challenge LEA decisions and whose child's Statement is ultimately re-written by the Tribunal in a way that is consistent with the law. In the other, much larger, group are those who do not challenge and as a result end up with inadequate statements which fail to guarantee provision for their children.

That many LEAs routinely either break or ignore the law was made clear by the Audit Commission in 1992 and again in a number of submissions to the 1996 Select Committee. Unnecessary strains are put on the Tribunal when LEAs make decisions that are inconsistent with the law. Since the Department for Education and Employment has shown itself reluctant to intervene in individual cases where parents have a right of appeal to the Tribunal, parents have no remedy other than appeal. It is not surprising that it is the most articulate and confident parents who have led the way. The real issue is how to support the less confident so that remedies obtainable only through appeal are open to all.

The issue of entitlement

As the impact of Tribunal decisions has begun to be felt in LEAs, so the whole question of entitlement has started to be debated. Under the 1993 Education Act, as under the 1981 Act, LEAs have duties and consequently children, while not having rights, have entitlements. LEAs have four main duties:

1 they must identify whether any child 'has special educational need' and 'it is necessary for the authority to determine the special educational provision which any learning difficulty he may have calls for' (1993 Education Act, section 165);

2 they must assess a child who falls, or probably falls, into the above category (section 167).

3 if, following an assessment under section 167, it is necessary for the LEA to determine the special educational provision which the child needs, the LEA must 'make and maintain a statement of his special educational needs' (section 168: 1). The Statement must 'give details of the authority's assessment of the child's special educational needs' and 'specify the special educational provision to be made for the purpose of meeting those needs' (section 168: 2). The regulations, which are statutory, go on to define the contents of the Statement, which should 'in particular specify ... any appropriate facilities and equipment, staffing arrangements and curriculum' which are necessary to meet the child's needs (Schedule B, Education (SEN) Regulations 1994);

4 They must arrange the special education provision specified in the Statement (section 168: 5).

For the first time, with the new Tribunal system, parents have access to appeal panels which are familiar with the law and are robust about applying it. The effect on LEAs has been dramatic, as submissions to the Select Committee showed. As a result, LEA submissions to the Select Committee also reflect a growing movement to create new legislation which would dismantle entitlement completely.

The likely impact of such a change has been explored by the present author elsewhere (Simmons 1996a, b). To summarise, the removal of entitlement would place children with special needs in the same situation as that currently experienced by the elderly and the long-term sick. Without entitlement, children, like the elderly, might find themselves assessed by LEAs who then had no obligation to meet their needs. The removal of entitlement would be likely to expose children with special needs to the vagaries of local politics, with locally established criteria of need which would take away from them the guarantee that their identified needs would be met. Further, though opponents of the current system might argue that replacing current legislation might lead to 'fairer' division of limited resources, it would still leave the most articulate able to use the system most effectively, without the framework of the law to support those who lacked the ability to make an effective case.

The elaboration of such a debate lies in the future: as the Tribunal becomes established and the impact of its judgements is assimilated, the movement to dismantle the legal entitlement of children with special educational needs is likely to gain momentum. Preserving entitlement is likely to be one of the main concerns of the voluntary sector over the next few years. Those anxious to present the case for entitlement will need to show that taking existing legal protection away from the most vulnerable members of society will not create a system that is any 'fairer' than the existing one. They will need to convince legislators that the real issue is to ensure that all children, not just those whose parents are able to make effective use of the tribunal system, have access to that entitlement.

Conclusion

The Special Educational Needs Tribunal has brought about great changes in the way that LEAs discharge their obligations to children with special needs. It is likely that in the future the impact of the Tribunal will act as a catalyst to yet more changes. Though hope was expressed at the outset that Tribunals would not be confrontational perhaps it was inevitable that they would serve to polarise the two parties involved. It may be that the existence of the Tribunal is fundamentally at odds with the notion of promoting partnership. Certainly a number of clear issues have already emerged as a result of the Tribunal's work which have direct relevance to developing partnership with parents.

One of these issues must be the role of individual professionals who, employed by LEAs, might be called to give professional evidence about the child's needs and the provision required to meet those needs. It appears that in some LEAs those professionals are neither free to write Advice in the way that the law intends nor able to speak freely at Tribunal hearings. In such circumstances, any potential partnership between professionals and parents has to be under threat, since the parent would be obliged to use a summons to require attendance at a hearing and to put the professional on oath while giving evidence. Professionals who are trying to implement the Code's perspective on partnership with parents may find their integrity compromised and their credibility undermined if they are not able to be honest with parents about childrens' needs in the discussions leading up to LEA decisions.

Secondly, the issue of representation is yet to be confronted by the voluntary sector. In 1992, the Audit Commission pointed out that parents supported either by a lawyer or by the voluntary sector tended to be more satisfied than others who were unsupported. The new law has not changed that situation. Parent partnership officers are rarely able to support parents at hearings; few parents can afford lawyers. If all parents are to have access to the Tribunal process, then the voluntary sector must develop strategies for training and supporting more advocacy workers. Without growth in advocacy work, Tribunals will continue to remain largely inaccessible to unsupported and less confident parents.

Action is needed from the Department for Education and Employment to prevent unnecessary appeals against LEA policies that are inconsistent with the law. Such action would ensure fairness for all. It cannot be equitable that in some LEAs only those parents who appeal to the Tribunal can have Statements that meet legal requirements. The Tribunal hearing should be the forum for honest disagreement, not the place where Statements are rewritten in accordance with the law.

For some parents, appeal to the Tribunal has brought an opportunity to ensure that their children receive the provision to which they are legally entitled. Where partnership has failed to deliver this entitlement, the Tribunal has often succeeded. Even with the Tribunal in place, parents are likely to face continued struggle to ensure that their children's needs are met. They will continue to need informed support and representation in order to make the best use of the new system. But in the end, it may be active advocacy, rather than partnership, which brings Tribunal decisions within reach of all parents.

References

Andrews, E. (1996) *Representing Parents at the Special Educational Needs Tribunal.* IPSEA, PO Box 1933, Marlow, Bucks, SL7 3TS.

Audit Commission (1992) *Getting in on the Act.* London: HMSO.

Education Committee (1996) *Special Educational Needs: the working of the Code of Practice and the Tribunal.* Session 1995–96. Report together with the Proceedings of the Committee, Minutes of Evidence and Appendices. London: HMSO.

Croall, J. (1994) 'Hope on Appeal', *Guardian Education,* 1 March.

Pyke, N. (1994) 'Needs Tribunals Set for Flood of Appeals', *Times Educational Supplement,* 25 February, p.8.

Simmons, K. (1996a) 'Entitlement to Special Needs Must be Preserved', *Times Educational Supplement,* 8 March, p.15.

Simmons, K. (1996b) 'In Defence of Entitlement', *Support for Learning,* 11, 3, pp.105–8.

Special Educational Needs Tribunal (1995) *Annual Report.* London: HMSO.

10 The needs of children and families: integrating services

Vincent McDonnell

The earlier chapters of this book have offered a series of personal experiences and professional reviews of the progress that has been made in working towards the concept of a collaborative service for children with special educational needs in partnership with parents. In this chapter, some of the policy implications for local authorities and health authorities will be discussed, reflected against the increased demand all agencies are experiencing for assistance and in a climate of budgetary controls that are, by necessity, leading to a culture of case prioritisation for all agencies.

The motivation to collaborate

All those who work in the public sector recognise that inherent financial pressures have highlighted the need to collaborate in making the most efficient and effective use of the resources available. However, for many, the more compelling reason to change traditionally recognised approaches to planning and delivering services is found in a collective recognition of the mix of difficulties facing many families and children in need. For those involved in the planning of services, the challenge facing them becomes not simply to agree on which set of complementary but competing needs have priority, but to rethink how the range of services to be offered is provided for and funded.

Dessent (1996) reminds us that 'partnership', like virtue, is by definition a good thing. Whilst this is undoubtedly true, when the three most significant agencies of Health, Education and Social Services are working within in a national framework in which they vie with each other for the annual allocation of public sector funding, there is a need to have a clearly identified, reciprocal understanding of each other's definition of need if such goodness and virtue are to prevail. As we are all aware, there is a national movement to promote the positive process of Children Services Plans, as referred to in chapter 1. The paradox for local service providers is that alternative national legislation mitigates against specific required outputs of such a planning process. The move to increase the level of devolution of budgets and delegation of associated responsibilities to all agencies means that, in reality, it is frequently left to the individual service provider to determine the critical needs of an individual case and how these needs are going to be met. An increasing emphasis on the philosophy of internal markets, self-governing trusts and encouragement of delegated fundholders can often restrict the opportunity to identify an agreed common criterion to determine a priority risk.

Whilst agencies may aim to develop a new culture among the 'human services', characterised by comprehensive integrated response to pupils' needs, it is a reality that, despite the best efforts of all those involved, separately funded and separately administered services, working to different legislative frameworks often produce more conflict among the differing professionals than many would care to admit to families, for whom the services may already seem confused and fragmented. Though the solutions to the difficulties many pupils face cut across a range of services, each agency has to identify its overall service priorities in meeting the needs of the wider community that it serves, whilst simultaneously reviewing the needs of any individual child or family.

So it is that the historical approach to service delivery has often served to divide the different services into departments or agencies, each with its own separate mandate, policies, procedures, philosophy, legislation and funding mechanisms. These inadvertently act as actual barriers to the collaborative approach applauded by government. Recognising this, it is important to emphasise that initiatives for introducing change may flounder as much through the manner in which funding is centrally identified as through the reluctance of localised professionals.

Those who work to alleviate the primary care, health and educational needs of young people in need frequently overlap in the planned provision they seek to offer – yet conflicting strategies may actually block any specific proposals to form a care or educational plan. If asked, many care workers, health workers and teachers would agree with Davis and McCaul (1988):

> We know what works! This is not the problem. Rather, the real problem lies in our individual and collective failures to apply what we already know to help our most troubled and troubling young people in a comprehensive, intensive and well-coordinated manner.

Barriers to collaboration

Is it the case that all the barriers to change are seen to be outside the control of those who have daily contact with children and families? Can all resistance to change be justifiably attributed to service managers, who in turn shield themselves within a cloak of the overall service delivery, determined by locally elected members and reflecting the legislative demands of a national framework? It is no criticism of those who care for some of our most needy young people that direct caseworkers, regardless of discipline, may find themselves caught up in such a debilitating cycle of 'defence' when services fail to live up to the expectations of families. Simply, there are a number of inherent barriers that need to be reviewed if change is to be realised.

Structural barriers

- agency mandates and definition of service provision
- lack of appropriate levels of resourcing to meet perceived need
- differing philosophies and perspectives among services
- absence of collective case management responsibilities between differing services and within job descriptions of staff members
- government funding procedures and programmes
- lack of protocols for collaboration between organisations
- organisational financial needs prevailing over individual case needs.

Human barriers

- heavy workloads and demands that leave little time for exploring new approaches
- lack of awareness, training and information
- protective attitudes towards case priorities within organisations
- lack of experience of working within a collaborative framework
- historical approach to service and business planning among services, government and localised agencies.

Whatever the balance of responsibility we may place on each agency to breakdown these barriers, we cannot escape a view that, though the major services providers recognise that children's needs should be met as part of a whole process, there is an inherent weakness in casework management that leaves a responsibility within and between services to compete for time, attention and funding on behalf of their own caseload. As Davie (1993) highlights, the prevailing system that services and families work within is actually loaded against multi-professional collaboration.

> If one were to attempt – with all the insights derived from research and common experience – to establish a process designed to keep the professional apart, it would have been difficult to conceive of any improvement on what we currently have.

The daily reality facing many a beleaguered caseworker, medical practitioner or educationalist is a sense of frustration, bewilderment and disappointment that colleagues from other agencies do not seem to recognise the self-evident difficulties that are so clearly manifest from their own perspective. How often has a medical representative suggested residential school as best suited to meet a child's difficulties, without identifying a proportionate share of funding? Or a teacher believes a family needs to be supported by social services, yet the family does not meet the case criteria determined by the Social Services Department? These are realities that must be reviewed and openly discussed if matters are to progress. In the present climate, the difficulties for any single 'professional' in realising an agreed, shared series of achievable goals that respond to the pressing concerns of the individual, could actually be a source of pressure for the caseworker equal to the confusion, distress and friction experienced by many families with children in need.

There is a widely reported perception that a growing number of pupils are coming to school with a complex range of social, emotional, behavioural, health and developmental difficulties that are creating barriers to learning. Teachers' efforts to teach and the abilities of children to learn are felt to be impaired by a growing number of pupils who are seen to have unmet social, emotional, health or physical needs. Factors that place children at risk are frequently interrelated and usually more than one issue is impacting on a child and family. Yet we still have to acknowledge that we must not only change the systems and structures that impact on a family, but also examine the attitudes and values of each service in prioritising service delivery.

For those involved in education, it is frequently the breadth of social disadvantage or emotional adjustment that, when set alongside the demands of current education legislation, forces them into a series of new alliances with the other statutory agencies. That is to say, the difficulties for many pupils are becoming so significant that, without the added benefit of the extended family and infrastructure of social care that existed within previous generations of families, new social legislation has been introduced to replace the often lapsed social or community–based structures of support that were historically available.

The needs of families within the community

Whilst there is an argument that the decentralisation of government funding removes the blame for service shortcomings from central government to localised purchasers, those who have had the opportunity to be involved in shaping the delivery of locally defined services would suggest that it carries with it many positive advantages. However, for services to collaborate, members of the respective services have to feel they will gain more from supporting such an initiative than they will by focussing on their own priorities of case or pupil needs. There is no point fighting shy of the fact that services can go about their business responding to the needs of their clients, largely independent of each other without needing to meet together or work closely together. Though the outcomes of shared working practices can be positively significant for the family, the benefits can be minimal for the agencies concerned. Ultimately, if a close working relationship is to operate successfully, it must be in the interests of both the family and the agencies as well (Dessent 1996).

In the past, such success was frequently achieved by education, health and social services negotiating, almost by default, through families or communities. The cultural change witnessed in the 1990s has meant that the family or community structures that may have once responded to the particular caring or social needs of individual families or children are no longer clearly evident. Increasing numbers of single parent families, social mobility, medical advancement and new legislative demands are symptomatic of the argument that there is now a level of expectation placed upon the main agencies that did not exist historically. So it is that the allegiances being forged between service agencies, in statute as well as through evolution of practice, could well be seen not only as an indication of collective growth in knowledge and understanding but also as a reflection of a new assessment of the individual's needs within a different construct of the family or community.

Whilst the range of responses offered to a perceived individual need may vary, it is clear that the response to the needs of some of the most needy and vulnerable families demands that coordination of services spreads beyond any singular case or any individually assessed need. It is for the greater good of society as a whole as well as of local communities that a wish to change and develop services must be firmly established at the heart of identifying the conditions to affect change. A review of possible contributions, roles and responsibilities for each of the organisations involved in meeting the needs of a clearly defined community may then offer an answer that national legislation, promoting collaboration, fails to recognise. Carers and families should become active partners in the determination of the service delivery to meet the needs of the children, with families themselves offering some moderation to the hierarchy of locally perceived needs. What is more important is that such an approach would not only place the user in a position of evaluating service delivery, but would also ensure they will share a responsibility for the outcomes – bringing us back to a culture of a local community caring for its own needs. This would strengthen the capacity of families and communities to determine their own needs, reestablishing the principle that the well-being and development of children and their families are the focus of the move towards a sharing of collaborative responsibilities, reflected in locally agreed patterns of spending.

Put more directly, in order to ensure that the families and children with the most significant levels of need are supported, we need to develop an approach to the delivery of public services where this is clearly recognised and debated. One of the reasons parents and families may feel dissatisfied with the service they receive from any single agency is that national policies may well have raised expectations. Thus carers expect an agency outside the family to be in a position of being the main provider of support. There is a collective need to move away from this almost exclusive position to a continuum of support that, quite legitimately, believes and declares children are usually best served in the context of their own family – and families in the context of their own communities. Children and families should have access to the necessary services that will allow them to achieve equity, but in an enabling capacity that will strengthen their ability to operate independently, through the various agencies and by virtue of ensuring access and self-sufficiency. Increasing the involvement of families, service agencies and voluntary or community services in defining the issues and implementing locally determined solutions provide the opportunity for a more sensitive understanding of the issues. This will encourage more relevant, community-based solutions that broaden the spread of locally-based financial and personnel resources that contribute to the assessment of need.

Adopting such an approach would, by necessity, lead to a fresh examination of the manner in which funding is identified, ensuring the funds available match local needs. It would include an assessment of the number of clients needing access to the highest level and the full breadth of coordinated services available, through to those who need no more than advocacy or partial access to assistance in order to meet their own needs successfully within the community. The movement towards a more collaborative service delivery and the planning of such integrated services will then be based on community-identified needs and cooperative action at the community level. In some areas, such as more rural areas, gaps in services may become apparent as the examination of service delivery unfolds. In such cases, the community that faces the shortfall can identify the key players and then work through the local and national agencies to identify a more effective allocation of the available resources.

No longer can we simply assume the continued pattern of service delivery we have historically expected. We need to rethink how services are and can be provided within a community. We need to consider how communities, government and non-governmental agencies can work at a level that more immediately recognises the varied services and support necessary to support the child and the family to retain their place in their community.

Integrating services through schools

As discussed earlier, the historical approach to service delivery has been to fund and divide different services into the agencies we have come to accept. There is also an acceptance that the factors that place children and their families at risk are interrelated. Placing the focus on the needs of a community and the 'families-of-need' within the community, will allow for the future planning of services that will work towards a comprehensive, responsive but above all accessible style of service delivery, the lead being taken by locally-based service providers.

In many families with a special educational, social or care need, one of the most constant forces in the lives of these families is the school. Because of the expectation that children with need will, as with all pupils, attend school, the school is the one place where the child is in regular attendance. For the most part, these families will maintain significant contact with school, particularly as they would have a number of opportunities to review the progress their son or daughter is making. School is also a point of reference for a range of agencies outside education to turn to, as they look to ensure recorded checks are carried out – for example health checks or vaccinations. There is a strong case for defining 'community' by reference the pivotal role of the school and families' commitment to the development of their children through the work of the school. From this beginning, the movement towards an integrated, school-based series of services becomes easier to grasp as a shared concept or vision. It is already a tangible reality for schools and could easily become accepted as a methodology for all locally based workers.

Using the school as a base from which services for children in need are delivered to the community, we would see a new approach to the planning of services, offering health, social services, housing and all other associated services the opportunity to meet families in an environment that many families see to be at the very heart of their local community. The participation of these agencies, which extend beyond the mandate of the school but whose participation has a significant impact on the lives of the families in the school, will inevitably have a beneficial effect on the existing systems and structures, as well as in attitudes and values.

In applying these principles, it is not suggested that the service agencies maintain a constant, daily place in school that replicates an office or base that may already be available. Rather, the parents and carers of children with special educational needs would know that, on a regular basis, a representative of the housing department, or a welfare officer, social worker or school nurse would be available in school to offer advice and support to the families of some of our most challenging young people. A health agency worker or social worker might well challenge the economics of such a proposal, criticising the possible impacts workloads or suggesting that such arrangements might serve the needs of education but not help them in their daily work. Accepting that most pupils will only spend approximately 25 per cent of their week in school, such arguments have validity. However, the critical factor is that the time in school is a constant time of regular attendance with a predictability that allows other agencies to benefit from families' involvement with schools. In a culture that offers a single agency focus with a service rather than client system, it is both predictable and understandable that 'other' agencies outside education would require full involvement and consultation if they were to be persuaded. Integrating services through a school is not about delivering services with some small modifications aimed at enhancing coordination. It is about a fundamental change in the way in which we think and work.

Integrating services through the school as a base is about:

- a broad-based community involvement
- addressing the needs of children through a constant organisational approach.
- finding ways of making better use of existing financial and human resources
- building coordination and collaboration into everyone's profession
- revised organisational systems that empower field staff to search out locally-based responses
- flexible structures within an organised framework that promotes ownership of the decisions made
- community-based responses to the collective needs of the children and families identified as being in need.

The legislative framework through which services work would then reflect the above change. Community or school-based participation and ownership would be agreed within local government or health trusts, providing an overall vision, policy and coordination, hopefully removing structural and other barriers.

If there is a fault that could be exploited within the collaborative delivery of services being discussed here, it is that the families who would benefit from the approach being promoted are already 'known' to the services. How could agencies whose first priority was not education ensure that they were still meeting the needs of their client groups, if there was a requirement to focus on service delivery through school? By way of response it is not an exclusive model of service delivery that is being proposed, but a 'surgery' or 'clinic' approach to agency collaboration that would see such a positive conclusion.

The managers of health and social service agencies would collaborate with teachers and other educational professionals to share information and coordinate services, agree case management conclusions and create opportunities to understand more fully what each agency can or cannot do to best meet the needs of all concerned. It is not intended that this would supersede other priority casework, single service initiatives or service budgetary management, all needing to remain with staff in whom formal responsibility for a service delivery is invested. The interpretation of the interagency collaboration suggested here would allow conflicting demands to continue in harmony. The essential difference is that the families with need, who make up such a significantly high proportion of the regular caseload for the service agencies, would see harmonisation of services more clearly evident at a local service level.

Working for the future

Change on the scale discussed here will take time to realise. To promote and see much of this work through to a conclusion we all need to commit ourselves to a new culture, characterised by cooperation and a new definition of service delivery. In many ways we will be entering territory that is familiar in principle, if more remote in practice. Whatever our starting point, it is a journey that we will only be able to make successfully if there is some centralised agreement about service priorities and a common understanding of how individual cases are identified for support.

It is clearly evident that all centrally-funded services are receiving an ever-increasing number of requests for support and assistance. The reasons for this increase are discussed elsewhere, but they include increased levels of knowledge, a perceived increase in the levels of need within society and structured changes in society resulting in a loss of the extended family. The consequence for the main services is that families have an ever-increasing level of expectation that centrally-funded services will fulfil their individual and family needs. With constant pressure on the level of funding made available centrally to deliver services, there are occasions when, to everybody's regret, agencies and families end up in conflict. Fundamental, then, to both the proposals outlined here and the daily delivery of services is a sense of realism and honesty. This will ensure that, whilst services always endeavour to be as responsive as possible to the needs of all, there is a clarity of service provision that does not allow families or service providers to be lured into a false sense of security through the belief that more funding is available than is the case.

There are many outstanding examples of good practice between agencies, families and the voluntary sector, as exemplified elsewhere in this book. In all honesty, such practice often arise from the willingness of individuals within communities or interest groups to make services work in collaboration, rather than from clear policy decisions, consciously taken. Where it works well, local initiatives use the process of service delivery to create partnerships among schools, communities and central agencies. The sense of purpose that characterises their work relies on a willingness to recognise the complex needs of children and families within their own communities, against a clearly articulated and defined budget. So it is that, whilst finance plays a part, the more compelling motive to succeed is found in a need to identify and resolve the difficulties facing many children and families with special educational needs.

In considering the balance of support we make available to families, the objective of all service providers is to ensure that services are coordinated and integrated so as to be as comprehensive, responsive and flexible as possible. The points raised for discussion in this chapter are intended not only to provide some clarification of current difficulties, but also to point in the direction we need to go to meet future challenges. In conclusion, there is an open invitation to all agencies to share resources and responsibilities, in order to break down the barriers to learning, and thus to enable children with special educational needs to succeed in school and in their home life.

References

Davie, R. (1993) 'Implementing Warnock's Multi-Professional Approach', in Visser, J. and Upton, G. (Eds) (1993) *Special Education in Britain After Warnock*. London: David Fulton.

Davis, W.E. and McCaul, E.J. (1988) *New Perspectives in Education: A Review of the Issues and Implications of the Regular Education Initiative*. College of Education, University of Maine.

Dessent, T. (1996) *Meeting Special Educational Needs – Options for Partnership Between Health, Social and Education Services*. Tamworth: NASEN Publications.

Index

e United Kingdom
Source UK Ltd.
0004B/445

9 781853 464294